SURVIVING THE TRIBULATION

Surviving the

TRIBULATION

Are You Equipped for the End Times?

Pat Benedetto

Deep River
B O O K S

Things of great sorrow and renown have come to pass.
Shall we weep or be glad?

J.R.R. TOLKEIN

ISBN: 9781940269405

Library of Congress: 2015933420

Cover design by David Litwin

Printed in the United States of America

CONTENTS

Part Two
SURVIVAL STRATEGIES

INTRODUCTION

When I was a child in the 1950s, the world seemed like a fun, exciting, and safe place, full of opportunities. Growing up in New York City, I was protected by my family, a quaint and cozy neighborhood, and a non-intrusive, mostly trustworthy government. Going to church or the synagogue was a given. The streets were safe enough that my mother could send me to the Italian bakery six blocks away for a daily loaf of bread when I was just seven years old and an adolescent could take a train downtown alone. Doors didn't need to be locked. Adults would gather outside in the evenings to watch baseball or play cards, while children played hopscotch and waited for the ice cream man with his happy jingle.

But as I changed, I noticed the world changing, too.

I think it may have started in the sixties with the Age of Aquarius. Or maybe with the Industrial Revolution or the Age of Technology. But after much study and reflection, I realize that it really began in the first days of our home called Earth. In the Garden of Eden, humanity chose its destiny and every day since then has been moving us forward to a final conclusion.

If you are reading this, you are probably curious about end-time events, expecting the Tribulation to occur in the near future, or actually living in the strangest and most terrible time that has ever befallen planet Earth.

The Tribulation is the last seven years in the history of the world as we know it. This period is the culmination of thousands of years of revelation, promises, hope, and knowledge that ultimately brings about final redemption. It will not be pleasant but a necessary test that will determine our eternal destiny. *Then there will be a time of anguish greater than any since nations first came into existence* (Daniel 12:1 NLT).

The very word *tribulation*[1] is synonymous with trouble and distress. Unfortunately, we're all acquainted with that scenario! Trouble and tribulation visit every human being at one time or another in the course of a lifetime. During those times, our security is shaken, our freedoms are taken, and our faith we can't be fakin'!

"In the world you will have tribulation, but be of good cheer, I [Jesus] have overcome the world" (John 16:33).

Time is of the essence, so I will try to be concise. In the two parts of this book, I hope to accomplish a few things: (1) to explain what is happening, (2) to prepare you for unfolding events, (3) to comfort you in a time of distress, and (4) to point you to the Source of all hope.

I won't be here during the Tribulation period, thanks to an amazing event I will tell you about later. However, it is possible many will survive this terrible time to populate the Kingdom.

Speaking of which, I hope to meet you there!

Part One

WHAT ON EARTH IS GOING ON?

Chapter 1
THE MASTER PLAN

I am convinced that God does not play dice.

ALBERT EINSTEIN

S ome things are a mystery. As human beings in this current age, we cannot fathom all of the secrets of the universe. However, many things were revealed to us: (1) how we came into existence, (2) why we are here, (3) what happens when we die, and (4) where history is heading.

This revelation comes in the form of the nature that surrounds us, including our physical selves and the universe; the Bible, which is the instruction manual given to humans; and the manifestation of God as Jesus Christ, who is written of in the history books and still makes Himself known today.

His story (or history) goes something like this.

God is one God (I AM), consisting of three persons: the Father (called Yahweh or Jehovah), the Son (Jesus Christ), and the Holy Spirit (inexplicable and yet wholly intimate as He lives inside believers and may be the "computer" that keeps track of every thought and action, is the very essence of love that comforts us, the author of all wisdom, our worship leader, and so much more).

The Trinity is hard to comprehend, so we've been given glimpses of the three-in-one concept in the material world: gas/liquid/solid; red/yellow/blue; proton/electron/neutron; body/soul/spirit; length/width/height (a three-dimensional plane we live within). Poor analogies, for sure, when compared to the awesomeness of God. He is one God in three persons— united in purpose, truth, power, and love, who never changes and is omniscient, omnipotent, omnipresent, that is, all-knowing, all-powerful, and everywhere.

Before He made man, God created angels—special beings to serve Him. They were given free will, as humans would later have. Under Lucifer's prideful leadership, a third of the angels rebelled against God. They became known as "fallen angels" or demons. *How you are fallen from heaven, O Lucifer, son of the morning!* (Isaiah 14:12a).

But even with the angels to serve Him, God decided He wanted to love and to be loved in return. So God said, *"Let Us make man in Our image, according to Our likeness; let them have dominion over the fish of the sea, over the birds of the air, and over the cattle, over all the earth and over every creeping thing that creeps on the earth." So God created man in His own image; in the image of God He created him; male and female He created them* (Genesis 1:26–27). Earth was created for mankind to live in and mankind was created to glorify God. He didn't want puppets that could only do what He wanted but rather friends who would freely choose to love Him and have a relationship with Him.

Besides Jesus, we are the central characters in a great cosmic drama.

So God put the man and woman in the Garden of Eden (somewhere around present-day Iraq) and told them to tend it. Adam and Eve enjoyed fellowship with God as He walked with them in the cool of the day, and experienced perfect health, peace, and fulfillment. But God gave them just one stipulation: they could eat the fruit of any tree except for the Tree of the Knowledge of Good and Evil. *The LORD tests the righteous* (Psalm 11:5a).

Lucifer was jealous of the love that God bestowed on man and prideful of the worship man gave God, so he decided to destroy Adam and his wife, and all mankind who would follow. Lucifer, former angel of light, became Satan, ruler of darkness and the great deceiver.

He slipped into Eden and asked the woman, *"Did God really say you must not eat the fruit [of the Tree of the Knowledge of Good and Evil] in the garden? ... God knows that your eyes will be opened when you eat it"* (Genesis 3:4–5 NLT).

Human nature chooses wrong every time. We want what we can't have. We rebel against rules and authority. We question God's motives. We are prideful and egotistical. Humans weren't created defective because God proclaimed creation "good," but rather it is our free will that is rebellious and disobedient, thwarting God's original plan and proving that only God is, indeed, good. *No one is good—not even one* (Romans 3:10 NLT).

Eve thought the fruit looked delicious and, now that the idea was presented to her, she wanted to be smart like God. So she ate it and gave some to Adam, and he ate also. Suddenly their eyes were opened and they knew they were naked, afraid, and ashamed. They would live out their lives in toil and trouble until the day their bodies returned to the earth. All of nature would be cursed, and innocence would be lost. Disobedience (sin) caused a chasm between the natural and supernatural, as God asked, "Where are you?" Of course, He knew where they were, but God wanted them to see the effects of their decision. They hid from Him! Humans were banished from the Garden.

But God loved the humans so much that He had a Master Plan already in mind. He said to Satan, *"From now on, you and the woman will be enemies, and your offspring and her offspring will be enemies. He will crush your head, and you will strike his heel"* (Genesis 3:15 NLT). This was a riddle that would become clear as history wore on.

Humans turned out to be a tough crowd. The people who populated the earth grew increasingly evil. They killed their brothers, fornicated with demons, worshiped idols, sacrificed their children, stole from their neighbors, and were generally wicked and corrupt. *So the Lord was sorry that he ever made them. It broke his heart* (Genesis 6:6 NLT).

God wiped everyone out in the Great Flood, sparing just righteous Noah and his family, along with enough animals to start over. Not long after, He destroyed Sodom and Gomorrah when the few righteous people were disgusted by the tremendous sin they saw all around them. But throughout Scripture we see God's great love reaching out with mercy and forgiveness.

God called out a group of people to concentrate His love on—the people of Israel through Abraham, Isaac, and Jacob—and guided them to the Promised Land. He gave His law in the form of the Ten Commandments to Moses. God performed great miracles and provided for them but people, even the Israelites, could not be perfect and holy like God. They, too, had the sinful nature that causes a chasm between God and man, separating us from Him. *For all have sinned and fall short of the glory of God* (Romans 3:23).

Because *the wages of sin is death* (Romans 6:23), mankind was required to kill an unblemished animal as a substitution for him or her self. This was a blood sacrifice that would foreshadow the ultimate final sacrifice of a Messiah who would, once and for all, save the people from their sins. And then at the appointed time, the Son of God and Man was born in Bethlehem. He was called Jesus, the Christ, the Anointed, Messiah, Emmanuel, Light of the World, God with Us, the Morning Star, Redeemer, Wonderful, Counselor, Lamb of God, King of Kings, Lord of Lords, Alpha and Omega, the Word.

In the beginning was the Word, and the Word was with God, and the Word was God. He was in the beginning with God. All things were made through Him, and without Him nothing was made that was made. In Him was life, and the life was the light of men (John 1:1–5).

During His time on the earth, Jesus was able to show us what God is like because He was God incarnate—God in flesh. Strong yet loving; just yet merciful. He healed the sick who came to Him, drove out demons, turned water into wine, multiplied loaves and fishes, raised the dead, commanded the wind and the waves, and taught us the things of God. But most of all, Jesus lived a sinless, perfect life and became the Lamb of God who would take away the sins of the world when He died on the cross. Delivered by the Jews, crucified by the Romans, but actually sent there by every last one of us because we are all sinners for whom a big debt needed to be paid.

It's very interesting that when the Roman governor, Pontius Pilate, brought out Jesus and a murderer named Barabbas, in an effort to make the crowd decide who should die and who should go free, they yelled, "Give us Barabbas." They called for innocent Jesus to be crucified and the bad guy to go free. The word "Barabbas" means "son of a father," which technically is Everyman or woman.

You see, God is just and needs to punish sin, but He is also love and wants to save us. On the day He died, Jesus became our substitute and took on the punishment for our sins. The veil in the Temple that separated the Holy of Holies from the people was torn in two. The debt had been paid and fellowship with God was restored. God's wrath was satisfied. This was the Perfect Plan. *For God so loved the world that He gave His only begotten*

Son, that whoever believes in Him should not perish but have everlasting life (John 3:16).

That would've been enough. But on the third day, just when Satan thought he had the victory ("striking the heel"), Jesus rose, resurrected from the dead, to prove that He had power over death and Satan, to reveal what happens to us after we die, and as evidence that the Father accepted His sacrifice as a substitute for our sins. Thanks to Jesus, we are forgiven and our debt has been paid!

In the present time, anyone who truly believes that Jesus is the Son of God in human flesh and that He died for his or her sins is saved and indwelt with the Holy Spirit, our Helper and Comforter, as we join with His Body, which is the Church. We are gifted with eternal life in heaven—a beautiful place beyond our imagination where we will enjoy an immortal body, fellowship with others, joy forever, and the presence of God and the angels. Those who don't accept His sacrifice (and are thus considered wicked) will be resurrected to eternal death in hell, a place of horror, torment, loneliness, thirst, despair and, yes, wailing, and gnashing of teeth. *"So it will be at the end of the age. The angels will come forth, separate the wicked from among the just, and cast them into the furnace of fire. There will be wailing and gnashing of teeth"* (Matthew 13:49–50). It's our choice.

The Shroud of Turin is a linen cloth bearing the negative photographic image of a man who suffered physical trauma in a manner consistent with crucifixion. Some contend that the shroud is the cloth placed on the body of Jesus Christ at the time of His burial and the image was "burned" by the light and energy of the Resurrection. To date, the body image visible on the Turin Shroud has not been explained by science.

The past two thousand or so years have been the Age of Grace—the Church Age—when all that is needed to be saved is to believe that Jesus is exactly who He said He is. All believers who have died during the Age of Grace (and whose souls have been waiting in Paradise) are united again with their physical bodies and raised together with the believers who are still alive in an event referred to as the Rapture. (This will be discussed in detail in Chapter 4.)

The Tribulation is the last seven years before the Second Coming of Christ to the earth. It is a time unlike any other, filled with deception and chaos, false peace and false christs, natural and supernatural catastrophes, fear, and sorrow. The time when God judges the nations, pours out His wrath on an unbelieving world and demands that everyone make a decision for Him or against Him.

After the seven years of Tribulation, at the culmination of the Battle of Armageddon, Jesus returns with all of His saints and angels to defeat the Antichrist and cleanse what's left of the earth to set up His Millennial Kingdom, a time of beauty and peace. The lion will lie down with the lamb. The thousand-year reign of King Jesus ends with the Great White Throne judgment, a.k.a. "Judgment Day." Unbelievers will be sent to hell and believers will step into eternity in the New Heaven and New Earth, where we will live happily ever after.

With such a grave future, how important is it for you and your loved ones to accept Jesus today? How urgent is it to get this message out to others? *Today is the day of salvation* (2 Corinthians 6:2b NLT).

Redemption is near, so hang in there and keep your eyes on the prize!

Chapter 2
BASIS OF TRUTH

The truth is more important than the facts.

FRANK LLOYD WRIGHT

Truth is not a relative term. In reality, there can only be one Truth. Ponder this: 1+1=2 and not 5. It never equals 5 even if you think it does, even if you believe it to be so. You may not believe in gravity, but it exists nevertheless—and it must exist. It doesn't matter if you know it or not, like it or not, or even care about it. Jump out of an airplane without a parachute and you and gravity will meet up.

It's the same with spiritual truth. Different religions can make up any god of their choosing, from a golden calf to Allah, but calling something god does not make it God. If these gods act, expect, reward, and teach differently, they all can't be right! There is, and can only be, one reality and anything else is either ignorance or deception.

If man were to think up the perfect god, he would want one who is merciful, all-powerful, just, loving, and trustworthy. Those qualities easily fit the God of the Bible. But mankind could never, in a million years, think up a God who loves His creation enough to stoop down to the earth to show us the way, and to suffer and die for our sins so that we can be together in fellowship. God became one of us and, by His resurrection, we can know without a doubt that there is life after death. That is an amazing and unique thing!

CREATION

God is the Creator of the whole universe and that truth is evident in the creation. Just as a building has a builder and a painting has a painter, creation has a Creator. *For since the creation of the world His invisible attributes are clearly seen, being understood by the things that are made* (Romans 1:20a).

Every rainbow is a sign of His promise never to destroy the earth again by water; every human body is a miracle of engineering. Snowflakes are common yet each one is an individual design. Caterpillars morph into butterflies to teach us about the resurrection; the plant cycle parables reaping and sowing; the myriad variety yet uniqueness of the animal world showcase His creativity.

The truth of God in creation really hit home for me when I visited Butterfly World. Along with the many live insects fluttering around the enclosure was a museum with dead bugs tacked to an exhibit. Each butterfly had the most beautiful colors and designs on one side, with a completely different color scheme and design on the other. The Blue Morpho butterfly gets its name from the iridescent blue that is actually reflected light from microscopic scales on the wings, while the underside is a camouflage brown pattern to help hide from predators. In flight, the contrasting blues and browns give the impression of appearing and disappearing!

"Ask the animals and they will teach you. Ask the birds of the sky and they will tell you. Speak to the earth and it will instruct you. Let the fish of the sea speak to you. They all know that the LORD has done this" (Job 12:7–9 NLT).

Or what about laminin? Merriam-Webster defines it as a "glycoprotein component of connective tissue basement membrane that promotes self adhesion." It is the glue that holds us together and, get this, it's shaped like a cross! *He [Jesus] existed before everything else began, and he holds all creation together* (Colossians 1:17 NLT).

DNA (deoxyribonucleic acid) is an organic double helix that carries our genetic code and is a fundamental element of heredity. It contains the instructions used in the development of all known living organisms and predetermines our physicality. Since DNA is a code, something or someone with serious brain power had to create it. Intelligent design, indeed.

Laminin

Man expands his mind for knowledge and God fills it. As we search ever further out in the universe or magnify the smallest particle, there is something there. Mathematics is so precise and expansive that only God could organize it all. There is an amazing example called the Fibonacci numbers (or sequence) that has been called the fingerprint of God. Each number in the sequence is the sum of the previous two numbers, with the first two numbers being 0 and 1. It goes 0, 1, 1, 2, 3, 5, 8, 13, 21, 34, 55, 89, 144, and so on. This ratio is found in almost every aspect of nature, from the multiplication of amoeba or rabbits to the spirals found in flower petals, pine cones, the nautilus seashell, and even the galaxy. A Creator has His hand in math.

The beauty and strange language of music is otherworldly and impossible to comprehend without God. It's amazing how many millions of songs have been written from seven basic notes. How many different songs do you know? Or how about the millions of colors blended from the seven colors of the prism? You can even narrow it further to just the three primary colors. C'mon.

Water alone is a miracle to me—its many uses, interesting properties, availability, and its necessity for all life. Our human bodies defy evolution. It's been said that it takes more faith to believe that we evolved from a single cell than to believe that we were created by intelligent design. The best gloves in Macy's can't outperform the skin and dexterity of our fingers. Ponder your eyeball. A tiny bird is nothing like a human. I haven't seen any half-monkey, half-man creatures. How can evolution explain this?

And on the earth, the power unleashed during certain weather events boggle our minds and scare the wits out of us. Amazing, complex beauty can be found in a seemingly unimportant flower. Our natural world points to a Creator.

THE GOSPEL IN THE ZODIAC

Then God said, "Let there be lights in the firmament of the heavens to divide the day from the night and let them be for signs and seasons, and for days and years" (Genesis 1:14).

Did you notice the word "signs?" There is a fascinating and remarkable witness of the truth (technically a part of creation) that has been told in the night skies since the beginning of time. If you look at the civilizations of Greece, Rome, or even further back to Egypt, Assyria, Babylonia, or Persia, every one has a description of the major stars in the heavens, known as the Constellations of the Zodiac or the Signs of the Zodiac. All civilizations had the same twelve signs, representing the same twelve pictures, placed in the same order. Historians and archeologists have deciphered hieroglyphics, uncovered stone tablets, searched ancient books, and still cannot discover how it is that they all contain the same signs!

Even stranger is that the stars representing the twelve signs don't seem to resemble the pictures of the signs themselves. For example, the constellation Ursa Major (the Great Bear) doesn't look like a bear at all, even with some lines connecting the dots (stars). So where did the signs come from? The evidence points to the fact that God Himself drew the pictures and actually named them! *He counts the number of the stars; He calls them all by name* (Psalm 147:4). *The heavens tell of the glory of God. The skies display his marvelous craftsmanship. Day after day they continue to speak, night after night they make him known. They speak without a sound or a word; their voice is silent in the skies; yet their message has gone out to all the earth and their words to all the world* (Psalm 19:1–4 NLT).

In the book of Job, which is thought to be the oldest book of the Bible, God says, *"Can you bind the cluster of the Pleiades, or loose the belt of Orion? Can you bring out Mazzaroth in its season? Or can you guide the Great Bear with its cubs?"* (Job 38:31–32). The word Mazzaroth means "the constellations of the zodiac" in Hebrew.

According to Arabic tradition, Seth and Enoch were the founders of this ancient understanding of the heavens in which salvation was foretold, that is, the Seed of the woman would destroy the seed of the serpent. *"By His spirit, He hath garnished the heavens; His hand hath formed the crooked serpent"* (Job 26:13 KJV). One of the largest of the constellations is called "The Crooked Serpent."

Granted, a study of this subject is a bit too complicated for the purposes of this book, so I'll give you just one example.

Sagittarius is at the center of our galactic system. It is pictured as a two-natured creature; much like Christ is both God and Man. He's an archer, aiming his arrow directly at the heart of Scorpio, the Scorpion. It's common knowledge and biblically affirmed that Satan is referred to as a snake, serpent, dragon, and scorpion. There are smaller stars within each constellation that further clarify its meaning. Complicated yes, but an amazing depiction of the Truth. (For further study, see *www.zodiactruth.com* or *The Real Meaning of the Zodiac* by D. James Kennedy.)

The corruption of this awe-inspiring zodiac began as far back as the Tower of Babel. The great deceiver, Satan, never wants humans to discover the truth and so concocted counterfeit stories that turned the stars into astrology and the pictures into mythology. Instead of trusting in Christ to which the stars point, modern astrology says to trust in the stars themselves. Instead of pictures telling the story of the gospel, Greek mythology made them into false gods. This is why God hates astrology. *"You have more than enough advisers, astrologers and stargazers. Let them stand up and save you from what the future holds. But they are as useless as dried grass burning in a fire"* (Isaiah 47:13–14 NLT).

Just as a star led the three Wise Men to the stable where Jesus was born, pure astronomy leads us to the truth of a Creator and the Gospel message.

THE BIBLE

The Bible claims to be the only inspired Word of God, which is the account of God's actions in the world and His purpose with all creation. It took more than fifteen centuries and approximately forty human authors to complete sixty-six books with very different styles, yet all containing a cohesive message. It utilizes narratives, dialogues, proverbs, parables, songs, genealogies, allegories, poems, history, and prophecy.

Critics have attempted to discredit the Bible by attacking its authority, credibility, and relevance. Recently, books and movies that twist biblical stories into something altogether different have been popular. It's astonishing how people can accept an even more absurd story rather than investigate the literal interpretation the way it was written. Because when we actually study the Bible for ourselves, it becomes obvious that it is not just another book—it is the Living Word. Libraries are full to the rafters with books, but the Bible is unique among them all. It is a storehouse of accounts in which we recognize the failures and triumphs of ordinary people—our very own stories.

If we can believe that the Bible is literally a handbook from God Himself to His own creatures, it becomes a powerful and awesome thing. It would contain the Truth of all that we seek.

Some of the evidence for the Bible's claims:

• TIME-TESTED. If the Bible had a fatal flaw, somebody would have found it by now after thousands of years of scrutiny. Atheists, scholars, intellectuals, and theologians have examined every verse seeking something to disprove its divine inspiration. It has outlasted governments that sought to ban it and skeptics who have sought to burn it into oblivion. The rather recent finding of the Dead Sea Scrolls confirmed what was already gathered. The Bible remains the best-selling book of all time (per the *Guinness Book of World Records*). *The grass withers, the flower fades, but the word of our God stands forever* (Isaiah 40:8).

• SCIENTIFIC EVIDENCE. Every new discovery only confirms the facts found in the Bible. References to almost every aspect of our world is covered, from the earth being a sphere (Isaiah 40:22) to ocean currents (Psalm 8:8) to embryonic development (Job 10:10-11) to healthy dietary rules (Leviticus 11:9–19) to the hydrological cycle (Job 36:27–28, Amos 5:8b) to the jet stream (Ecclesiastes 1:6) to laughter promoting healing (Proverbs 17:22) to dinosaurs (Job 40:15–24) to the origin of music (Psalm 40:3) to plant processes (1 Corinthians 15:36–38) to soil conservation (Leviticus 25:3–5) to astronomy (Amos 5:8a)…and so on! Archeology has only reinforced the proof of Bible truths, confirming the Red Sea crossing, Noah's ark and worldwide flood, the temple in Jerusalem, the empty tomb, and more. There is such an abundance of evidence that there's even a magazine called *Biblical Archeology*. In fact, no legitimate archeological discovery has ever contradicted the Bible!

• NO EDITORS OR PROOFREADING SOFTWARE. Another amazing fact

is the Bible was put together without the help of editors or publishing houses. Any proofreading would've been done by comparing every single character with human eyes—without the assistance of modern software such as spell check.

The Old Testament canon was accepted by the time of Jesus. *"These are the words which I spoke to you while I was still with you, that all things must be fulfilled which were written in the Law of Moses and the Prophets and the Psalms concerning Me"* (Luke 24:44). The New Testament was debated by a few; however, it is crucial to remember that the early church did not decide what would be included. It was God and God alone who determined which books belonged in the Bible. The human process may have been flawed but God, in His sovereignty, brought the early church to the recognition of the books He had inspired. (See *The Canon of Scripture* by F.F. Bruce for more info.)

The Bible was written in three languages: Hebrew, Aramaic, and Greek. All major translations transpose from the original language, which means it hasn't been translated from Hebrew into German and then into French and then into English. Each language is translated from the original. The first English-language Bible in America was the King James Version. The Bible was the first book reproduced on a printing press.

The scribes who copied the early Hebrew manuscripts were very much aware that they were doing sacred work and exercised the greatest of care. Not only did they count the words but each character to be sure they hadn't missed even a "jot or tittle."

I believe that an omnipotent God easily has the power to sustain and protect the integrity of His book. The mighty Holy Spirit of God inspired inferior man, whether directly or indirectly, to pen the words that He wanted us to know. *We know these things because God has revealed them to us by his Spirit, and his Spirit searches out everything and shows us even God's deep secrets* (1 Corinthians 2:10 NLT).

• TESTIMONIES AND WITNESSES abound in corroborating the Bible, or relating how it changed and affected lives. The historians Flavius Josephus, Pliny the Younger, and Tacitus wrote about Jesus as an actual person, confirming His actions in the New Testament, His resurrection, and the persecution of the early Christians. The Bible's influence on literature, music, and art is matchless. On his deathbed, Sir Walter Scott requested, "Bring me the book!" When asked, "What book?" he replied, "There is but one book!" Isaac Newton accounted the Scriptures to be the "most sublime philosophy with more sure marks of authenticity than in any profane history book whatsoever." Queen Victoria gave the Bible credit for the British Empire's successes. And Andrew Jackson, the seventh president of the United States, said, "That Book is the rock on which this republic rests." Nobel Peace Prize recipient and Holocaust survivor Elie Wiesel has observed, "An inspired work, the Bible is also a source of inspiration. Its impact has no equal."

Time itself has been divided by the humongous impact of the birth of Jesus, the main focus of the Bible. Jesus Himself quoted from the Old Testament. With His words *"From the blood of Abel to the blood of Zechariah..."* (Luke 11:51), Jesus confirms His witness to the Old Testament canon from A to Z.

There are far too many historical and famous people with pithy quotes and insightful commentaries to mention, but they express the importance of the Bible and the great love they have for its precious words.

• PROOF OF PROPHECY is perhaps the strongest argument for the authenticity of the Bible. A true prophet is 100 percent accurate and past biblical prophecies have been fulfilled to the letter, giving us confidence that the prophecies for the future will come to pass as well. *And so we have the prophetic word confirmed, which you do well to heed as a light that shines in a dark place until the day dawns and the morning star rises in your hearts; knowing this first, that no prophecy of Scripture is of any private interpretation, for prophecy never came by the will of man, but holy men of God spoke as they were moved by the Holy Spirit* (2 Peter 1:19–21).

The Old Testament contains approximately 300 references to the Messiah that were fulfilled in Jesus Christ with the remainder to be fulfilled at the Second Coming. Isaiah 53 describes the life of Jesus 700 years before He was even born!

Here are just a few examples of the Old Testament prophecy and its New Testament fulfillment:

1. The Messiah would be born in Bethlehem. (Micah 5:2; Matthew 2:1)
2. The Messiah would be born of a virgin. (Isaiah 7:14; Matthew 1:18-23)
3. The Messiah would be a descendant of David. (Jeremiah 23:5; Revelation 22:16)
4. Herod would attempt to murder the Messiah. (Jeremiah 31:15; Matthew 2:16–18)
5. The Messiah would be betrayed by a friend. (Psalm 41:9; John 13:18)
6. The Messiah would be sold for thirty silver coins. (Zechariah 11:12; Matthew 26:15)
7. The Messiah would be crucified. (Zechariah 12:10; John 19:16–18, 37)
8. Lots would be cast for His clothes. (Psalm 22:18; Matthew 27:35)

A most amazing prophecy that, to me, seals the deal is Daniel's "seventy weeks" proclamation (Daniel 9:24–25). Using a 360-day year, he predicted that 173,880 days would elapse between the decree to rebuild Jerusalem (by Artaxerxes in March 14, 445 BC) and Messiah the Prince (April 6, 32 AD). According to most calculations, when Jesus rode into Jerusalem to shouts of "Hosanna," the first 483 years were fulfilled to the day (more on this subject later).

God doesn't want His children to be ignorant so He warned them beforehand of the fate of cities and impending judgments. The destruction of Sodom, Gomorrah, Nineveh, and Jerusalem were prophesied before the fact. Noah spent about a hundred years trying to convince the world that he wasn't crazy for building an ark because God told him what would happen ahead of time. Through dreams, God foretold to Daniel and Joseph the things that would be. The impetus and inspiration for this book are the prophecies that speak of the future. I've seen many of these predictions already come to pass with my own eyes.

The great philosophical questions of mankind—Who am I? Why am I here? What happens after I die?—are answered in the Bible. It is a refuge in times of trouble. People in pain, in prison, in mourning have found strength there in their most desperate hours. It is a guide for living life to the fullest and direction through the tempestuous voyage of life. It anchors us in the storms that inevitably come our way, is a strong foundation when the world we know disappears and when the din of this world confuses us. Its words beckon us to listen to the very heart of God.

THE LIFE OF JESUS

Since Jesus Christ is the The Way, The Truth, and The Life, then the basis of Truth resides in Him. I would not suggest that you give your life to a person that you do not know; to ask that you serve a master who you do not respect; to obey a Lord who has no power; to worship a God that you do not love; to put your faith in a Messiah who cannot save; to believe a tale that is not true—so following is a brief overview of One Amazing Life.

His story is not just found in the words of the Bible but has been corroborated in extra-biblical texts. The Jewish historian Josephus wrote in 93 AD, "About this (previous) time arose Jesus, a wise man. He drew to himself many; and when Pilate, on the indictment of the principal men among us, had condemned him to the cross, those who had loved him at the first did not cease to do so. And even to this day the race of Christians, who are named from him, has not died out."[2] Cornelius Tacitus, a Roman historian, wrote Annals in 112 AD, which is accepted as a strong indicator of Jesus' existence in the early first century. Men from different cultures who wrote about the reality and history of Jesus include Eusebius of Caesarea, Tertullian, Agapius, Justin Martyr, Pliny the Younger, and Philo of Alexandria. The Hebrew Talmud (the Bible's Old Testament) prophesied about His coming and purpose. Don't allow revisionists who twist the past to rob you of the very fact that Jesus really walked on this earth.

Eyewitnesses are always the most reliable source of information. These would be His friends, family, apostles, disciples, and the healed and awestruck masses. The New Testament of the Bible begins with the eyewitness accounts of Matthew, Mark, and John. The Gospel according to Luke begins, *Many people have set out to write accounts about the events that have been fulfilled among us. They used the eyewitness reports circulating among us from the early disciples. Having carefully investigated everything from the beginning, I also have decided to write a careful account for you, most honorable Theophilus, so you can be certain of the truth of everything you were taught* (Luke 1:1–4 NLT).

Jesus came to the earth as a baby boy in the small town of Bethlehem in, well, approximately the year 1 AD (Anno Domino, the year of our Lord). His life was so important that it changed the entire calendar and the marking of time started over! (During the Tribulation, the Antichrist changes the "times and seasons" so your calendar may be some other format. The humanists of today refuse to call it AD and instead call it CE or Common Era.) *Then the angel said to them, "Do not be afraid, for behold, I bring you good tidings of great joy which will be to all people. For there is born to you this day in the city of David, a Savior, who is Christ the Lord"* (Luke 2:10–11).

Jesus descended from Adam through Seth, Enoch, Noah, Abraham, Isaac, Jacob, David, and Joseph, et al. Mary was a virgin when she conceived because a mother of God needed to be pure and Jesus already had a Father—making Him both God and Man! Her fiancé Joseph was told the situation in a dream so he would accept and protect her and the child. When Mary's pregnancy was far along, they were forced by Caesar Augustus to return to Bethlehem for a census. While there, Jesus was born under a special star with a multitude of angels saying, *"Glory to God in the highest. And on earth, peace, goodwill to men!"* (Luke 2:14).

The family settled in Nazareth where Joseph taught Jesus the carpentry trade. In Jerusalem at the age of twelve, Jesus sat in the Temple with the religious leaders and impressed them with His knowledge. *Now so it was that after three days they found Him in the temple, sitting in the midst of the teachers, both listening to them and asking them questions. And all who heard Him were astonished at His understanding and answers* (Luke 2:46–47).

Jesus' public ministry began at the age of thirty after being baptized by John the Baptist and defeating Satan's temptations in the wilderness using

Scripture. He called twelve men to be apostles in His inner circle—and invited a few others, including women, as close friends and disciples.

Miracles attracted crowds who were then more receptive to what Jesus had to say. His first miracle occurred at a wedding feast in Cana where He and His mother were guests. The steward had run out of wine, so Jesus told the servants to fill up six pots with water and, when the steward drew it out for the master of the feast, it was wine—and the finest wine at that. Jesus had compassion and healed everyone who came to Him of various sicknesses: the blind could see, the deaf could hear, and the lame could walk. He raised a little girl and Lazarus from the dead, proving that He was the Resurrection and the Life.

Having authority over the powers of darkness, Jesus exorcized demons from many unfortunate victims. *When He had come to the other side…there He met two demon-possessed men coming out of the tombs, exceedingly fierce, so that no one could pass that way. And suddenly they cried out, saying, "What have we to do with You, Jesus, You Son of God? Have You come here to torment us before the time?" Now a good way off was a herd of swine feeding, so the demons begged Him saying, "If you cast us out, permit us to go away into the herd of swine." And He said to them, "Go." So when they had come out, they went into the herd of swine. And suddenly the whole herd of swine ran violently down the steep place into the sea, and perished in the water* (Matthew 8:28–32).

Jesus also had authority over the forces of nature. On one occasion, He walked on top of the water toward the flabbergasted disciples in a boat. On another, He calmed a raging storm with just a word. He called so much fish into His disciples' nets that they were bursting when previously they couldn't catch any. And one day, after a day of healing and teaching, the disciples were concerned that the multitudes were hungry, wanting to send them away to the towns so they could buy food. But Jesus took five loaves of bread and two fish, blessed them, broke them into pieces, and passed them around. All ate (more than five thousand people) and were filled, and there were even twelve baskets of leftovers!

The wisdom and love of Jesus is evident in one of my favorite stories: *As Jesus was speaking, the teachers of religious law and the Pharisees brought a woman who had been caught in the act of adultery. They put her in front of the crowd. "Teacher," they said to Jesus, "this woman was caught in the act of adultery. The law of Moses says to stone her. What do you say?" They were trying to trap Him into saying something they could use against Him, but Jesus stooped down and wrote in the dust with His finger.* [I think He was writing their names and respective sins or the Ten Commandments.] *They kept demanding an answer, so He stood up and said, "The one who has never sinned throw the first stone!" Then He stooped down again and wrote in the dust. When the accusers heard this, they slipped away one by one, beginning with the oldest, until only Jesus was left in the middle with the woman. Then Jesus stood up again and said to the woman, "Where are your accusers? Didn't even one of them condemn you?" "No, Lord," she said. And Jesus said, "Neither do I. Go and sin no more"* (John 8:5–11 NLT).

Many of His teachings took the form of parables, a rather simple story that has a far deeper meaning, which He later explained more fully to the disciples. He told about the Prodigal Son, the Ten Virgins, the Sower and the Seed, the Faithful Servant, the Wedding Feast, the Mustard Seed, the Pearl of Great Price, and others. He taught us how we should treat government, *"Render to Caesar the things that are Caesar's, and to God, the things that are God's"* (Luke 20:25); treat others, *"You shall love your neighbor as yourself"* (Matthew 22:39); and to treat God, *"Whoever speaks against the Holy Spirit, it will not be forgiven him"* (Matthew 12:32). The Beatitudes taught us how to live, *"Blessed are the meek, for they shall inherit the earth" (Matthew 5:5).* His prophecies about the future read like today's headlines, *"For nation will rise against nation, and kingdom against kingdom. And there will be famines, pestilences and earthquakes in various places"* (Matthew 24:7). He explained how to pray, *"Our Father who art in heaven…"* (Luke 11:2) and how He saves us, *"Just as the Son of Man did not come to be served, but to serve, and to give His life a ransom for many"* (Matthew 20:28).

When the time came for Jesus to fulfill the prophecies and to accomplish the astonishing act that needed to be done to reconcile the world to God, it appropriately started on Passover in Jerusalem, where He instituted the Lord's Supper, or communion. *And as they were eating, Jesus took bread, blessed and broke it and gave it to the disciples and said, "Take, eat; this is My* body." Then He took the cup [of wine], and gave thanks, and gave it to them, saying, "Drink from it, all of you. For this is My blood of the new covenant, which is shed for many for the remission of sins" (Matthew 26:26–28). Afterward, He went into the Garden of Gethsemane to pray, so earnestly that He sweat blood—His flesh was weak and His mind fearful of the suffering He knew was next on the great agenda. But His spirit was strong enough to fulfill the Father's will.

Judas, one of the twelve, betrayed Jesus to the soldiers seeking Him with a kiss. The Jewish leaders had charged Jesus with blasphemy because He claimed to be God, and the Roman rulers didn't like that His followers were worshiping Him instead of Caesar. So during that night, He was handed over to Herod, who sent Him to Pilate, who washed his hands of Jesus' death to absolve himself of the guilt he felt. In reality we are all guilty; it was our sin that put Him to death.

The passion of Christ was a nightmare, a horrendous and brutal torture that involved a lashing with studded whips, a crown of thorns dug into His head, being spat upon, mocked, and forced to carry a heavy wooden cross up the hill to Calvary. The Passion. There He was crucified, crying out to the Father, "My God, My God, why have You forsaken Me?" (Matthew 27:46b). Even God, His Father, poured out His wrath for a sinful and rebellious world onto Jesus—the wrath that was meant for us.

Do you get that the King of the Universe and God Himself came to Earth as a human to sacrifice His life in place of ours—to be our blood sacrifice—so that we can be reconciled to the Father and have eternal life? What amazing love! When He died, the temple veil split, signifying that there was no more separation from God. The earth quaked and graves were opened.

Jesus was buried in a rich man's tomb. And on the third day, He rose from the dead, where He appeared to many before physically ascending into heaven. His final words were, "Go therefore and make disciples of all the nations, baptizing them in the name of the Father and of the Son and of the Holy Spirit, teaching them to observe all things that I have commanded you; and lo, I am with you always, even to the end of the age" (Matthew 28:19–20). He now sits at the right hand of the Father in heaven, interceding for the saints and looking forward to His Second Coming when all will be as planned and promised.

It's been said of Jesus: He went about doing good. That would make a noble epitaph for anyone. Jesus is more than a myth, a legend, or a super-hero, and much more than a prophet or great teacher. He came to the earth to show us who God is and to sacrifice His life for us. He is the personification of Truth.

And there are also many other things that Jesus did, which if they were writ-ten one by one, I suppose that even the world itself could not contain the books that would be written (John 21:25).

MY PERSONAL TESTIMONY

Appropriately, my testimony revolves around the search for The Truth. In 1970, as a teenager I was very influenced by the hippie culture—the fashion, the drugs and, especially, the music. In my growing, expanding mind, ever further from my nominal Catholic upbringing, I felt that life couldn't be lived unless you knew what was really going on. So I embarked on a search through all of the major religions and many cults as well. *"Seek and you will find, knock and it will be opened to you"* (Matthew 7:7b). *"Seek the Lord your God and you will find Him if you seek Him with all your heart and with all your soul"* (Deuteronomy 4:29).

The New Age almost caught me, but biblical Christianity was the only religion whose God loved me and desired a relationship with me! Only Christianity had the answers to all of my questions. Mohammed, Buddha, Gandhi, Confucius, and Abraham are still in their graves. Only Jesus Christ has the power over death.

After four years of study and contemplation, I was sitting in Vizcaya Gardens in Miami with an old friend who had become a Jehovah Witness. As she talked about their vision of the kingdom of God, suddenly a beam of sunlight fell on my face and I had this intense feeling that God was really real. Real like Truth.

God led me to reject the Jehovah Witness books and pick up The Living Bible translation. I spent a summer reading it from cover to cover, hardly able to put it down. Then I read it through again. Somewhere between verses and sometime during the summer of 1974, the light bulb went off as I wept and accepted Jesus as my Savior and Lord. I found a church and got baptized for real in a lake at Quiet Waters Park.

The proof of the Truth for me have been supernatural experiences where I just knew, without a shadow of a doubt, that God is real and He cares about me. Amazing things happen when God is involved, from an angel wearing a white, three-piece suit standing by a white Cadillac telling me not to worry and that "everything was going to be okay," to the IRS inspector forgiving a business mistake because of a dream he had.

Atheists mock Christians saying we have "an imaginary friend." Well, I've experienced God and it's not my imagination. I see God in a sunset or a smile. I feel Him in the touch of a lover, the warmth of a fire, the coolness of water, or the soft fur of my dog. The scent of Him wafts from a flower or envelops me in saltwater air or a pine forest. I hear His voice in the sweet strings of a violin and particularly in the quiet stillness. *"My sheep hear My voice"* (John 10:27a). My senses are full of the wonder of God. I speak to Him in prayer and He answers. He always shows up just in time.

In my life, I have experienced mountaintop highs, tender baby moments, fond childhood memories, adrenaline rushes, soul-stirring music, drug euphoria, orgasmic sex; however, the highest high I've ever experienced is when praising and worshiping God. Communing with the Lord induces complete satisfaction.

The reasons that I know Christianity is The Truth include, but are not limited to:

- Answered prayer
- Fulfilled prophecy, especially in my own lifetime
- Out-of-the-blue miracles
- The Word of God in the Bible
- Life, death, and resurrection of Jesus
- Confirmation of scientific principles
- Mercy, grace, blessings, and love
- Wonder and beauty of creation

- A feeling in my spirit
- The still, small voice of God

How can I not testify of the things of God? How can I not proclaim the plans He has for us? How can I keep quiet? *"When the watchman sees the enemy coming, he sounds the alarm to warn the people. Then if those who hear the alarm refuse to take action, it is their own fault if they die. They heard the alarm but ignored it, so the responsibility is theirs. If they had listened to the warning, they could have saved their lives. But if the watchman sees the enemy coming and doesn't sound the alarm to warn the people, he is responsible for their captivity. They will die in their sins, but I will hold the watchman responsible for their deaths"* (Ezekiel 33:3–6 NLT).

I feel the burden of being a watchman, and you have been warned!

The Bible, along with creation and the life of Jesus, express the Truth to men and women everywhere. *For the Lord is good, His mercy is everlasting, and His truth endures to all generations (Psalm 100:5).* And it is a frosted window where we can peer into the future and discern the signs of the times.

Chapter 3
SIGNS OF THE TIMES

"And now I have told you before it comes,
that when it comes to pass, you may believe."

JOHN 14:29

Signs are made to be seen. Traffic signs and signals point you in the right direction; a billboard is erected where it is hard to ignore. It's there, big as life, so you don't miss it.

God has used signs throughout history. He set the rainbow as a sign of His promise not to destroy the world again by flood, the increasingly painful plagues that showed the Egyptian pharaoh His power, and the sky sign of the Star of Bethlehem announced the birth of Jesus. Today, the signs increasingly point to His Second Coming. These events serve to wake us up to the lateness of the hour and to remind us that God has complete power over all the earth and that He has a plan!

Because God wills that none should perish, He always warns before executing judgment. And the warning signs are increasing in frequency and severity, like labor pains that ultimately come to fruition with the longed-for child. Labor cannot be controlled or stopped—once the process starts, nothing can stop it. Jesus said, *"But all this is only the first of the birth pains, with more to come"* (Matthew 24:8 NLT). Likewise, all of the events foretold, which we are now seeing, will worsen and become more frequent as history draws closer to the redemption of creation.

As with a billboard, a sign becomes clearer the nearer you get to it. The closer we get to the end of this age, the signs get increasingly more evident. *"You are good at reading the weather signs in the sky, but you can't read the obvious signs of the times!"* (Matthew 16:3 NLT). There are also clues to the future in the past; signs that were hidden until recent events or understanding shone some light on them. This is why interest in eschatology (the study of last things) has intensified lately.

Most of the prophetic warnings are concerning the Tribulation, so if we see those foretold events already happening, then we know the Rapture is that much closer. When you see the Christmas decorations in the department store, you know that Thanksgiving is right around the corner.

Many signs have been given to help us know when we are in the end of this age. Some find that reading the signs mentioned in biblical prophecy is scary business, but you know what's really scary? It's scary to see the craziness all around us and not know what happens or how it all turns out. It's scary to fall into the wrath of an angry God and not be covered by the blood of Jesus. That's why God has given us some details of what happens in the end because, like the old saying goes, "The devil you know is better than the devil you don't know."

We can walk in the light of revelation and not in the darkness of ignorance. And if we didn't know that there was some sort of conclusion to this mess called life, we would have no hope for a future. It would all be meaningless and incredibly sad. But, thanks be to God, we do have hope. And a happily-ever-after.

The beginning of the Bible reads a lot like its end. *History merely repeats itself. It has all been done before. Nothing under the sun is truly new* (Ecclesiastes 1:9 NLT).

We start with Creation and the Garden of Eden with mankind enjoying fellowship with God, and we end with the Creation of a New Heaven and New Earth with man again enjoying fellowship with God. Genesis 2 talks about the day of rest and that a thousand years is like one day to God, while in Revelation we learn about the thousand-year reign of Christ called the Millennial Kingdom, a time of rest and redemption. Ancient history describes the destruction of the Tower of Babel; recent history has the Twin Towers being destroyed. Enoch was taken to heaven before the Flood, just as believers are taken to heaven before the Tribulation.

Do you think what I'm saying is crazy? Then you are a fulfillment of prophecy, too.

Most importantly, I want to remind you that in the last days scoffers will come, mocking the truth and following their own desires. They will say, "What happened to the promise that Jesus is coming again? From before the times of our ancestors, everything has remained the same since the world was first created."

They deliberately forget that God made the heavens by the word of his command, and he brought the earth out from the water and surrounded it with water. Then he used the water to destroy the ancient world with a mighty flood. And by the same word, the present heavens and earth have been stored up for fire. They are being kept for the day of judgment, when ungodly people will be destroyed.

…The Lord isn't really being slow about his promise, as some people think. No, he is being patient for your sake. He does not want anyone to be destroyed, but wants everyone to repent (2 Peter 3:3–9 NLT).

Listed individually, there would be approximately a hundred signs, but I'm going to mention just a few and organize them by subject.

SPIRITUAL DECEPTION

Deceit is nothing new. In fact, it began in the Garden of Eden when Satan told Eve that she could be like God if she ate the fruit. Since Satan can appear as an angel of light, it's easy for people to be deceived into thinking they're experiencing miracles or speaking with dead people or seeing aliens to make us believe anything but the Truth. *"For false christs and false prophets will rise and show great signs and wonders to deceive, if possible, even the elect"* (Matthew 24:24). We need to test every spirit by the Word of God.

The last days technically started soon after Jesus returned to heaven, and it didn't take long for His words to get twisted and distorted. Roman Catholicism created their own rules and traditions, often contrary to the words of Jesus. For instance, reciting the rosary. *"When you pray, do not repeat vain repetitions like the heathen do"* (Matthew 6:7). As Christianity spread around the globe, it morphed into various denominations, as well as sects and cults who distorted, or distracted from, the original message.

It's getting harder to trust anything or anyone anymore—revisionists rewrite history books stating blatant lies, such as that the Holocaust never happened; the media spins stories to fulfill their own agendas; presidents and those in authority don't seem to be on their peoples' side and outright lie while putting through secret legislation. We used to say, "Seeing is believing," but that's not true anymore with computer graphics. Society believes lies and then perpetuates them until the lies are believed to be truth (separation of church and state?!). *But evil men and imposters will grow worse and worse, deceiving and being deceived* (2 Timothy 3:13).

For deception to occur, there needs to be a deceiver feeding the incredible lies and promoting the hoax. Guess who? Of course, the Great Deceiver and Father of Lies, Satan and his minions.

• FALSE CHRISTS. *"Don't let anyone deceive you. For many will come in My name saying, 'I am the Christ' and will deceive many"* (Matthew 24:5). Among those who have claimed to be the Messiah are Jim Jones, David Koresh, Sun Myung Moon, Jose Miranda, Adolf Hitler, Marshall Applewhite, Charles Manson, Inri Cristo, Allan John Miller, Lord Maitreya, and many others who exhibited manifestations of egomania, mental illness, or demon possession. Muslims are waiting for the Twelfth Imam or Mahdi, their version of a messiah who sounds eerily like the Antichrist. The Antichrist is the ultimate false christ who is possessed by Satan, preaching a different message than the Cross and demanding worship, dragging unwitting victims to the eternal pit.

• FALSE TEACHERS. *There will be false teachers among you. They will cleverly teach their destructive heresies about God…and make up clever lies to get hold of your money* (2 PETER 2:1–3 NLT). The early Catholic extortion of selling indulgences to pay for sins and a few television evangelists come to mind. Wayne Dyer distorts the truth and spews his New Age ideas, on public television! Cult leaders bend the truth just enough to damn all their followers, starting false religions like Scientology, Islam, Buddhism, Jehovah Witnesses, and scores more. An angel called Moroni supposedly visited

Joseph Smith, Jr. beginning in 1823, and gave him the source material for the Book of Mormon, the beginning of Mormonism. *But even if we, or an angel from heaven, preach any other gospel to you than what we have preached to you, let him be accursed* (Galatians 1:8).

Recently, there's been a plethora of books written by those who supposedly died and went to heaven; however, I have serious reservations about most of those books. One recommendation was so close to the Christian understanding of heaven until I realized that the author suggested that everyone goes to heaven if they just believe in God and His love. Well, even the devil believes in God! Not a word about sin, repentance, or the Gospel. Every day it gets harder to discern who is a true and who is a false teacher. We must be like the Bereans who search the Scripture daily to see if things are so (Acts 17:11).

• APOSTASY is a big spiritual sign for before and during the Tribulation. *For that Day will not come unless the falling away comes first* (2 Thessalonians 2:3). This could be referring to the Rapture (the "falling away" can also be interpreted as "coming out"), but there's no denying that today's culture is post-Christian. When I was young, it was just assumed that, if you were an American, you believed in God—whether Christian or Jew. Even rock songs in the seventies mentioned God as if He were a given. Now popular music blasphemes, ignores, or downright doubts God.

Now the Spirit expressly says that in latter times some will depart from the faith, giving heed to deceiving spirits and doctrines of demons (1 Timothy 4:1).

The saddest thing about apostasy is that a person can think he or she is a Christian and is going to heaven. Although I cannot judge any person's individual salvation, Jesus notes that there will be those who are surprised when they are turned away. *"Many will say to Me in that day, 'Lord, Lord, have we not prophesied in Your name, cast out demons in Your name, and done many wonders in Your name?' And then I will declare to them, 'I never knew you; depart from Me, you who practice lawlessness!'"* (Matthew 7:22–23).

Too many churches have moved away from sound doctrine and, frankly, I can't believe how fast that has happened. Some new church movements deny many core Bible teachings. *For the time will come when people will not endure sound doctrine, but follow their own desires and will look for teachers who tell them what they want to hear. They will turn their ears away from the truth, and be turned aside to fables* (2 Timothy 4:3–4 NLT).

The Prosperity message teaches that God wants every one of us to be healthy and wealthy to the exclusion of any suffering for Christ, and that it's only our lack of positive faith that hinders us. Some faith healers and charismatics use suspect (evil) powers to create an emotional scene that gets the people laughing uncontrollably, twitching, and writhing (eerily similar to what happens in kundalini yoga when the serpent at the base of the spine becomes energized). Beware of preachers who only want to make you feel good and never speak of hell or sin. Oh, and please send in your "seed" money.

Dominion Theology or Kingdom Now erroneously teach that the Church has replaced Israel in the covenant as they try to create a perfect world for Christ to return to, and they're getting downright militant about it. They think that things will get better; however, the Bible (and current events) teach us that things are getting worse, and will continue to get worse until after Jesus returns to the earth.

There's the Emergent Church, which actually denies that Jesus is the only way to heaven, being politically correct and accepting of all paths to God, a church for socialism. Their preachers write popular books about how to find purpose in your life, but never stress that Jesus said, *"I am the way, the truth, and the life. No one comes to the Father except through Me"* (John 14:6); or that *"Narrow is the way that leads to eternal life, broad is the way to destruction"* (Matthew 7:14). They feed the poor but not their souls. They sing praise songs but don't worship. They reject the truth for a lie. And why in the world would Jesus have had to die if everyone just went to heaven automatically?

The Ecumenical movement is hoping for religious unity at the expense of the Truth and is paving the way for global worship of the Antichrist who rules during the Tribulation. There is a conditioning or preparation for the global religion that begins with apostasy from the true faith towards the supposed greater good of tolerance and peace. The unification of world religions in the name of peace is a slippery slope. King Abdullah of Saudi

Arabia called for an interfaith dialogue saying, "If God wills it, we will meet with our brothers from other religions, including those of the Torah and the Gospel to come up with ways to safeguard humanity." Of course, it is likely that the true Christian faith, because it teaches only one way to God, will be viewed as intolerant and bigoted. Actually, that's already happening in a nation that has kicked God out of almost every public arena. Jesus was misunderstood and, so it seems, are His followers.

There is a word that has recently come to my attention: Chrislam. Yes, the blending of Christianity and Islam. At first I dismissed this concept because I thought those two religions were completely at odds with each other. However, according to the press service FIDES, on May 14, 1999, Raphael I Bidawid, patriarch of the Chaldeans, received Pope John Paul II and a Muslim delegation. At the end of the audience "the Pope bowed to the Muslim holy book, the Koran, presented to him by the delegation and he kissed it as a sign of respect for Islam." Pope Benedict and Pope Francis have offered olive branches to Muslims. The next (and possibly final) pope could conceivably be the False Prophet in a Revived Roman Empire.

On November 14, 2014 (the day after a Muslim imam for the Islamic Center of Central Jersey gave the opening prayer in the US House of Representatives), the National Cathedral in Washington, DC, invited the imam to lead prayers. They covered the crosses, removed the pews and laid down prayer rugs facing Mecca. A brave woman named Christine Weick traveled from Tennessee to DC and gained access to the cathedral. She stood up, pointed to a cross and shouted, "Jesus died on that cross. It is the reason we are to worship only Him. Jesus Christ is our Lord and Savior. We have built enough mosques in this country. Why don't you worship in your mosques and leave our churches alone!" It's very sad—and telling—that this was held in the National Cathedral, and I believe America will pay for this abomination.

The word "catholic" means universal. The reign of Antichrist will be global or universal. In Catholicism, Mary is revered and even worshiped as the Queen of Heaven, and she holds a prominent place in the Koran. In fact, the nineteenth chapter is named after her, being only one of eight people to have a chapter in the Koran named after them. In ancient Egypt, the false goddess Isis holds that title, and in ancient Mesopotamia, Ishtar also carries it. Mentioned in the Koran, the Midianites worshiped Ashteroth, also called the Queen of Heaven. *"The children gather wood, the fathers kindle the fire, and the women knead dough to make cakes for the queen of heaven;… that they may provoke Me to anger"* (Jeremiah 7:18).

• THE NEW AGE. This is the "religion" of choice for the rest of society—the ex-hippies, the globalists, atheists, agnostics, quasi-Buddhists, celebrities, progressive liberals, gays, occupiers, militant environmentalists, yoga enthusiasts, crystal gazers. The New Age movement started in the 18th century and gained momentum in the 1960s, taking influence from Indian gurus who brought their Eastern religious traditions to the West. It refers to an astrological Age of Aquarius and was brought to public attention with the popular musical, *Hair,* and chart-topping astrology books by Linda Goodman, both in the late sixties.

In the twenty-first century, environmentalism has fired up the New Agers. An Earth Charter was drawn up to reflect their conviction that radical change in mankind's attitudes is essential to achieving economic, social, and ecological success. This charter is housed in the Ark of Hope, a blasphemous fake copy of the true Ark of the Covenant. God's Ark held the Ten Commandments; this ark holds mankind's fist in the face of God, usurping His authority and elevating the creation above the Creator. What this signifies is that the Earth Charter becomes the new set of rules for the earth, pushing towards a one-world religion for a one-world government. After all, the earth must be saved, right? Not by us! Only Jesus can save our planet now.

• ALIENS. UFOs are Unidentified Flying Objects, and sightings of them have increased (according to a 1/13/13 Huffington Post headline, "UFO Sightings at International Space Station On the Rise"). It's curious that alien abductions began about 1947—approximately the time when Israel became a nation. The subject is shrouded in secrecy with government cover-ups, vague snatching stories, and unusual lights but no evidence of alien bodies or spaceships. I believe that UFOs are nothing more (or less!) than demons bent on distracting and deceiving us. Fallen angels can take form. There is a link between UFOs and occult phenomena, and studies indicate that these "aliens" act less like space travelers and more like demons, as they invoke fear, deliver anti-Christian statements, and transcend the laws of physics.

Recently there has been an increase in unexplained machine-like objects coming very close to the sun and unusual hovering lights seen in cities around the globe. These phenomena will become more common.

Most likely, aliens will be the explanation given as to where all those people went in the Rapture—aliens took them because they were unenlightened or some such lie. To the modern mindset, evolution is falling out of favor; however, alien "seeding" of our planet is preferable to the biblical account of creation to the fallen masses. Vatican astronomers are searching for extraterrestrial life, believing them to be just another part of creation. Not sure what day they were created on!

On the April 2, 2014, *Jimmy Kimmel Live* late-night show, former President Bill Clinton stated, "An alien invasion of planet Earth would not be surprising and could unite this increasingly divided world of ours." The Antichrist may even claim to be a space brother or ascended master coming to save our world. Do not believe any demon masquerading as an alien or some reptilian race from outer space! God makes no mention in His Word about creating other inhabited universes.

• THE OCCULT is tempting those who want to experience the supernatural and the dark forces are always eager to drag away another victim. Ouija boards, tarot cards, full moon festivals, Wicca, Satanists, psychics, drum circles, goddess worship, palm and tea readers, mediums, drug use, spirit guides, masochism, Santeria, and voodoo are acceptable practices. Just the other day, I was walking through the toy department of a megastore when I saw half an aisle devoted to a "game" with the word OUIJA in large letters—for ages 8+. When I was a child, a friend-of-a-friend had a séance, you know, for fun. She had a Ouija board, but even then, it felt creepy to me and I didn't participate. Parents may not realize that, by purchasing this so-called game, they are exposing their child to demonic influence and opening a doorway to the occult.

Haunted houses and ghosts titillate many. *"Give no regard to mediums and familiar spirits; do not seek after them, to be defiled by them; I am the Lord your God"* (Leviticus 19:31).

Vampires are now considered cool and sexy, and horror films are tops at the box office. The Wizarding World of Harry Potter is a popular theme park attraction, spawned from the best-selling book and movie series. Salem may not burn witches anymore but Burning Man festivals attract thousands. And what's up with all the talk about zombies?

> Since the time of the Second Coming is compared to the time of Noah, it's interesting to note that the world population at the time of the Flood has been calculated to be approximately 8 billion people. This large number was due to very long lifespans in the antediluvian atmosphere and the ability of each family to have many, many children. The population in 2015 is almost 8 billion people![1]

There is a mixed race of beings called the Nephilim, which are the result of a union between a demon and a human. *There were giants on the earth in those days, and also afterward, when the sons of God came in to the daughters of men and they bore children to them. Those were the mighty men who were of old, men of renown* (Genesis 6:4). These beings were just one reason why God destroyed the world with the great Flood, and God declares that before He returns, the world would again be like the days of Noah. *"And as it was in the days of Noah, so it will be also in the days of the Son of Man"* (Luke 17:26). It's probable that Satan's army is hard at work right now perverting and corrupting the human race again.

Pagan "gods and goddesses" from the demon world are making a comeback and influencing the supernatural realm in the following ways:

- Artemis—goddess worship, animal worship, animal rights, lesbianism
- Baal—oracles, polytheism, abortion, fertility
- Dionysus—drunkenness, Freudianism, ecstasy, pornography, lesbianism

- Eros—eroticism, mystic sex, body worship, body piercing, sacred prostitution
- Gaia—earth worship, environmentalism, paganism, pantheism
- Isis—Wicca, witchcraft, goddess worship, magic, channeling, visualization
- Vatchit—devil worship, channeling, visualization, necromancy

For we are not fighting against people made of flesh and blood, but against the evil rulers and authorities of the unseen world, against those mighty powers of darkness who rule this world, and against wicked spirits in the heavenly realms (Ephesians 6:12 NLT).

There is a creeping darkness spreading over our world. The Antichrist is the culmination of spiritual deceit and demonic power. The majority of the Tribulation population will believe that he is their messiah, but more on him later.

FAMINES AND PESTILENCE

Hunger and sickness are signs that hit us right where it hurts. We've all had experience with these attention-grabbers—we see them on the news, maybe donated to a telethon, know someone who is riddled with disease or doesn't know where their next meal is coming from. *"There will be famines and pestilences"* (Luke 21:11).

Famine has been around for a long time; however, it hasn't been until recently that it's become a global problem. Deforestation, natural disasters, industrial waste, and poor land management have destroyed farmlands around the world. Unusual weather conditions and agricultural diseases are wiping out crops, while water pollution is killing fish and seabeds. War interrupts the distribution of food. Millions of people around the world go hungry every day and their numbers increase every year. I recall posters of African children with their swollen stomachs reminding us that there were people on the other side of the world who weren't as fortunate. Now even Americans in the inner cities and back hills don't have enough to eat because of extreme poverty and isolation. Inflation is cutting into our grocery bills so that the elderly and unemployed are nutrient deficient. The prices for items have gone up while the portion sizes have gotten smaller. During the Tribulation, a day's wages will buy just a loaf of bread (Revelation 6:6).

The food we eat carries pestilence in the form of E-coli, salmonella, and other germs. Something is killing off the bees that pollinate crops and create honey. Animal die-offs and fish kills, with no known causes, echo God's words in Zephaniah 1:3: *"I will consume the fowls of the heaven and the fishes of the sea."*

The lack of food will only get worse as we head towards the New World Order. A UN Agenda 21 seeks to remove people from farms and bring them into cities where they can be better monitored. They say it's to protect the earth for sustainable development, but if you read the publication, it gives power to economic entities for controlling food. In the spring of 2012, US President Obama moved to ban all children from working on family farms until a national uproar caused him to rescind that idea. Farmers today are subject to so many regulations and increased taxation that they are leaving the family farms in droves. Drones patrol overhead and satellites spy to ensure compliance. Hunger games, anyone?

Pestilence refers to contagious diseases or deadly illnesses. Tuberculosis and polio, which were eradicated in the late twentieth century, are making a comeback. There have been epidemics of cholera, malaria, influenza, smallpox, and bubonic plague. Many people suffer from AIDS, SARS, STDs, MRSA, avian flu, swine flu, mad cow disease, West Nile, Lyme, enterovirus, Chikungunya, the dreaded Ebola, and more. We have flesh-eating bacteria and brain-eating amoebas.

Germs are mutating and becoming resistant to all known antibiotics and antiviral agents. Water supplies are becoming contaminated, causing water-borne illnesses in the poorer countries. Cancer most assuredly will take someone we know. Diabetes, heart disease, and autoimmune diseases are on the rise. Growing up, I couldn't name one friend who was sickly yet now it seems that more children are complaining of illnesses. There's an epic epidemic of sickness!

MASS ANIMAL DIE-OFFS

"There is violence everywhere—one murder after another. That is why your land is in mourning, and everyone is wasting away. Even the wild animals, the birds of the sky, and the fish of the sea are disappearing" (Hosea 4:2–3).

Strange things are afoot, my friend. Animals, mostly birds, fish, and marine mammals, but also bees, cows, and others have died mysteriously in mass quantities. This seemingly began November 2010 when thousands of sea birds were found dead in Tasmania, Australia. Then thousands of crows, pigeons, and other birds literally fell out of the sky—also in Australia. During the night of December 21, 2010, more than 5,000 blackbirds and starlings fell out of the sky in Arkansas. The birds were dead before they hit the ground.

The media has tried to gloss over these bird deaths as resulting from fireworks or illness; however, it was like God just snapped his fingers or gave the Word and down they went.

Whales and dolphins have been washing up on beaches around the globe. Thousands of dead crabs washed up on beaches in Chile. Thousands of dead fish were found in a harbor in Italy, another "cause unknown." Hundreds of chickens die suddenly in Indonesia. Some of these events may be due to an environmental issue or disease. Radiation from Fukushima could certainly be contaminating fish in the Pacific Ocean, and millions of bees could be dying from pesticides. They are happening, nonetheless.

Some statistics from the website *www.end-times-prophecy.org*, which include links to the actual news stories, show the following mass die-offs:

2011	141 events in 32 countries
2012	465 events in 67 countries
2013	798 events in 93 countries
2014	651 events in 76 countries

The third horse of the Apocalypse is the black horse bringing famine and death. With so many fish, pigs, chickens, cattle, and bees dying off, food shortages and high prices are inevitable. These poor innocent animals are dying because of mankind. It's because of our sin. Because we need something out of the ordinary—a sign—to wake us up to the reality around us. Do you think God is trying to tell us something? He is either warning us to repent or to discern the lateness of the hour—or both!

HUMAN DEPRAVITY

The litany of society's bad behaviors is long. *For men will be lovers of themselves, lovers of money, boasters, proud, blasphemers, disobedient to parents, unthankful, unholy, unloving, unforgiving, slanderers, without self-control, brutal, despisers of good, traitors, headstrong, haughty, lovers of pleasure rather than lovers of God* (2 Timothy 3:2–4).

Where to begin with this sign? Road rage. Name-calling. Bullies. Nowadays it's an oddity when a person is nice to us, when they hold the door for us, when they smile at us. The "Me generation" with self-help books, self-gratification, and careful-or-Johnny's self-esteem-might-get-hurt cannot afford to look at the needs of their fellow man. All this self-stuff has led to isolationism, vanity, greed, and a sense of entitlement.

The disrespect for our fellow man and those in authority is shocking. The 43rd President of the United States was verbally attacked in ways bordering on unreasonable and demonic. It's rare for kids to call their elders Mr. and Mrs. or help old ladies cross the street.

The police used to be considered helpful civil servants; now there are police killings—and police abuse. The unfortunate killings of black men by the hands of white police officers in Ferguson, Missouri, and New York City, among others, have incited a race war with riots in the streets, protest marches, and distrust of all law enforcement.

Littering. Cursing. Sarcastic put-downs. Not flushing a public toilet. Society has become cold as people ignore pleas for help, only concerned about themselves, afraid they may get sued or chip a fingernail. You could be dying on the street and bystanders will look the other way, or worse yet, video it for YouTube and Facebook.

Love your neighbor has been replaced by the love of self (humanism), the love of pleasure (hedonism), and the love of money (materialism).

The Internet, with its social networking sites, has created a generation of misfits without opportunities to develop face-to-face social skills. Hardly anyone knows their neighbor, much less offers to build them a barn, help them move, or bring them a pie. Kids rarely acknowledge you in a store or on the street. Too many people have their heads in a smart phone instead of experiencing the life going on around them. Memories aren't made playing video games!

Social networking, such as Twitter, has also allowed the formation of flash mobs who all agree to meet at a certain place at a certain time. It first started as harmless dancing in a train station or mall; however, now it's a gang of teenagers entering a 7-11 or other store, stealing, and knocking over items as they blow through. Angry youth are entering fast food restaurants and throwing food and chairs around and then exiting before the manager can react—and usually is afraid to act. According to police in Troutdale, Oregon, a group of forty teenagers stormed into an Albertsons grocery store on June 18, 2012, stealing merchandise and trashing the store. They said the kids walked en masse into the store and "flash robbed" the place —a play on "flash mob."

Violence in movies, television, magazines, video games, and sports all too often trickle into the streets

My generation (the so-called Baby Boomers) is the first generation that could practice effective birth control—surgical sterilization, latex condoms, the birth control pill—instead of the formerly relied-upon coitus interruptus or some herbal concoction. I am certainly not against birth control; however, it does disobey God's command to "be fruitful and multiply." Whereas former generations would have large families, today's families are much smaller with most couples opting for just one child. I see it with my own family tree—I have many more uncles and aunts than I have nephews and nieces.

and homes, causing emotional numbness so that killing doesn't seem like a big deal. Entire families have been wiped out in murder/suicides and a bad economy has fueled an increase in domestic violence (per the Police

Executive Research Forum).[2] Abortion kills too many unborn babies.

Rapes, carjackings, home invasions, brawls, drive-by shootings, mayhem, bombings, knockout attacks, gang warfare, and general lawlessness disrupt our feelings of security. Sloth, filth, squabbles, slanders, decadence, rebellion, incessant noise, self-mutilation, malice. Cannibalism is a new one here in the United States. A man in Miami ate the face off a homeless guy and, when confronted by police, he was naked with flesh hanging out of his mouth and growling. Growling! If that's not evil, I don't know what is. I've had just about enough.

Although animal abuse is nothing new, the escalation is alarming. Voodoo sacrifices, inhumane slaughterhouses, neglected barnyard animals, cockfights and dogfights, neighborhood ducks stuck with arrows, horses and greyhounds run to death, torturous testing, abandoned pets, general meanness, and disregard. My friend who is an Animal Control Officer relates horrific crimes against these mostly innocent creatures. (I say "mostly" because a few are so aggressive and mean that they just may be possessed!)

Is it any wonder why wild animals are increasingly attacking humans, which is another end times sign, by the way. *And power was given to them over a fourth of the earth, to kill with sword, with hunger, with death and by the beasts of the earth* (Revelation 6:8b).

Sexual immorality has steadily deteriorated since ancient days. Prostitution, the so-called oldest profession, is now rampant in most of the world and epidemic in some Asian countries. Human traffickers steal young girls and sell them into sexual slavery. Adultery and swinging are laughed at on top-rated TV shows—their innuendo is not lost on viewers. Teenage girls look for the love that their fathers never gave them in all the wrong places, hanging out with bad boys and getting "casually" pregnant or getting affection from other girls. A Japanese businessman makes love to (certainly not with) a fem-bot—a robot created for sex. Some coaches and priests molest little boys. Pornography is an addiction that only perpetuates an incorrect view of love and sex opposite to what God had planned as something beautiful and satisfying.

Homosexuality's affiliation with Sodom is a definitive sign. *"Likewise as it also was in the days of Lot…"* (Luke 17:28). The homosexual agenda is openly flaunted and forced upon our society. Gays and lesbians actually boast about their sin, parading it about town and demanding marriage rights. Transsexuals have become entertainment. Domination; degradation. Perversion can go as far as depraved minds will take it. This is an evil time, folks. *"Do not practice homosexuality, having sex with another man as with a woman. It is a detestable sin"* (Leviticus 18:22 NLT).

And what about lovers of money? *The love of money is the root of all evil* (1 Timothy 6:10 NLT). In America, there has been a problem of too much consumption (though the economy is in bad shape these days). A nice problem to have, some would say, but it has created a "gimme" monster. *You have heaped up treasure in the last days* (James 5:3b). We desire the latest gadget, the trendy clothes, a shiny new car, a bigger house. We work too many hours to obtain material stuff so that there's no time to eat together as a family. There are too many desires born of false advertising so that we spend our money on "junk" so there's nothing left for charities. We're too busy striving for the things that can be destroyed in a minute and that only distract us from eternal matters.

Gambling is a big problem for those who can least afford it. Too many are looking for the easy way to Easy Street, and you can pick up a lottery ticket or scratch-off at your local convenience store or try your luck at the casinos. Once I had to walk through a casino to get to a concert and noticed an elderly woman sitting alone, feeding $100 bills into the whizzing machine and pushing a button–over and over. It was very sad.

You can bet on the races, football games, or who will win the election. Love of money causes cheating on one's taxes, shady activities, family fights, envy, and a poor work ethic. We yell at the homeless on the street to get a job instead of handing over a dollar. Burglaries, robberies, looting, flash grabs.

There's no doubt in my mind that people are more fearful—I hear the anxiety in the voices of my friends and overhear it on strangers' cell phone conversations. Society has increasingly become gullible, blaspheming, and cold, isolating themselves behind walls, both real and imaginary. *The love of many will grow cold* (Matthew 24:12). Things seem upside down to me lately, as if I'm living in an alternative universe or something. *Destruction is certain for those who say that evil is good and good is evil; that dark is light and light is dark* (Isaiah 5:20 NLT).

A vast conspiracy is occurring to get everyone hooked on some type of pharmaceutical. TV commercials peddle the latest medicine that will "fix" us: children on Ritalin, women on Xanax, men on Viagra, and the elderly on daily cocktails of ten pills or more. Granted, medicine can be immensely helpful and lifesaving; however, with everyone "on" something, many will take the mark of the beast to continue feeding their addictions or fear of sickness.

There are other cultural signs that may not be considered depravity but do show an inclination away from God's best for us, such as shunning marriage (Catholic priests, Buddhist monks, and the majority of young people) and vegetarianism, *They will say it is wrong to be married and wrong to eat certain foods* (1 Timothy 4:3 NLT).

The famous philosopher, Pogo, remarked, "We have met the enemy and he is us."

CLIMACTIC OCCURRENCES AND SIGNS IN THE SKY

Our environment is probably God's most obvious way to get our attention. Hurricanes, floods, tornadoes, wildfires, droughts, blizzards, heat waves, volcanoes, avalanches, tsunamis—it seems every week there's a major weather story with meteorologists using words like biblical, epic, record-breaking, historic. In April 2011, according to The Weather Channel, a Super Outbreak caused 344 tornadoes in fifteen states with 321 fatalities, breaking the previous record. In March 2011, a 9.0 magnitude earthquake hit Japan—the most powerful in that nation's recorded history. Yes, Jesus said that a big sign would be *Earthquakes in various places* (Matthew 24:7 NLT). I researched the listing of earthquakes since they began keeping records and it is eye-popping how the frequency and intensity have increased just since 2002, and they've been appearing in widely diverse places all over the world. Tom Parsons, a research geophysicist with the US Geological Survey, said, "We have recently experienced a period that has had one of the highest rates of great earthquakes ever recorded."

Global warming has been a newsmaker, although now they're calling it climate change to justify the crazy weather in both directions that we've been experiencing. Environmental activists complain that humankind with all of our consumption is causing the earth to grow warmer, thus affecting every other aspect of our environment. It is true that man has not been the good steward of the earth as God intended, but it's getting plainer by the day that God's hand is stirring the climate to get our attention.

In May 2012, a violent hailstorm hit China, killing forty, collapsing 7,600 houses and destroying farmland. In June 2012 in the United States, 4,500 heat records were broken with many temperatures over 100°, tropical storm Debby caused unprecedented flooding, epic wildfires were burning in eight states, and a super *derecho* (a new one on me) swept from the Midwest to the Eastern Seaboard with winds that took residents by surprise. That's in one month, in one country alone! Too cold, too hot, too much rain, not enough rain, hailstones the size of softballs, fast-moving fires, sinkholes swallowing up large houses—are you awake yet?

I realize that nature has seen its share of tragedies since the beginning, but the frequency and intensity (birth pains!) of events are prophetically significant. Naysayers mention that it's because of increased communications that we are now aware of these events; however, I'm talking about big news that would make its way around to at least the historians, almanac keepers, and scientists. We knew of the destruction of Pompeii before the Internet was invented!

Significant Worldwide Earthquakes

per United States Geological Survey
http://earthquake.usgs.gov/earthquakes/eqarchives

Year	#	Year	#	Year	#	Year	#	Year	#
1138	1	1865	2	1914	2	1952	4	1986	4
1268	1	1867	2	1915	3	1953	5	1987	7
1290	1	1868	2	1916	2	1954	6	1988	4
1556	1	1871	3	1917	2	1955	1	1989	2
1619	1	1872	3	1918	4	1957	13	1990	3
1638	1	1873	1	1920	2	1958	4	1991	2
1663	1	1877	2	1922	2	1959	4	1992	4
1664	1	1879	1	1923	5	1960	4	1993	3
1667	1	1882	1	1925	4	1962	4	1994	2
1668	1	1884	2	1926	1	1963	3	1995	3
1687	1	1886	1	1927	4	1964	5	1996	1
1692	1	1887	2	1928	2	1965	5	1997	6
1693	1	1891	1	1929	4	1966	6	1998	10
1700	1	1892	2	1930	3	1968	5	1999	13
1727	2	1895	1	1931	7	1969	6	2000	6
1730	1	1896	1	1932	5	1970	5	2001	7
1746	1	1897	2	1933	4	1971	4	2002	45
1755	3	1899	6	1934	4	1972	3	2003	70
1780	1	1900	1	1935	7	1973	1	2004	48
1783	2	1901	3	1937	2	1974	4	2005	50
1791	1	1902	2	1938	3	1975	7	2006	33
1811	2	1903	2	1939	2	1976	7	2007	55
1812	5	1904	3	1940	5	1977	2	2008	41
1819	1	1905	4	1942	2	1978	1	2009	66
1821	1	1906	6	1943	5	1979	3	2010	89
1823	1	1907	3	1945	2	1980	1	2011	223
1835	1	1908	2	1946	7	1981	2	2012	146
1838	1	1909	3	1948	4	1982	1	2013	143
1843	2	1910	3	1949	5	1983	5	2014	156
1855	1	1911	4	1950	2	1984	1		
1857	2	1912	2	1951	4	1985	3		

In November 2013, super typhoon Haiyan hit the Philippines and was reported by CNN to be "one of the strongest storms ever recorded on the planet"! The same area suffered a 7.1 magnitude earthquake just the month before. That same month, seven volcanoes erupted in six countries just hours apart (Japan, Mexico, Guatemala, Vanuatu, Italy, and two in Indonesia). The media dubbed it "another doomsday omen."

"I will cause wonders in the heavens above and signs on the earth below—blood, fire and clouds of smoke" Acts 2:19 NLT). There are also to be signs in the sky, such as solar flares, alignment of planets, strange star behavior, comets that may or may not hit earth (you'd think that our advanced technology would detect these coming our way but many have whizzed by and surprised astronomers), meteors, blood moons, eclipses and halos, black hole and quasar discoveries, space exploration, and strange sights and sounds. Mystery booms have been heard in Wisconsin and around the world. Scientists can't seem to pinpoint the source. They even came up with a new name: skyquakes!

The American Meteor Society has logged the following meteor sighting statistical data: 692 sightings in 2009; 947 in 2010; 1630 in 2011; 2125 in 2012; and in late 2013 "re-

> 2010 NASA—A team of astronomers has detected a strange, cosmic noise that booms louder than expected. The roar is from the distant cosmos and nobody knows what causes it. There is "something new and interesting going on in the universe," stated NASA. ARCADE's mission was to search the sky for faint signs from first generation stars but instead they heard a roar from the distant reaches of the universe. Detailed analysis of the signal ruled out primordial stars or any known radio sources. *The Lord will roar loudly against his own land from his holy dwelling in heaven. He will shout against everyone on the earth, like the harvesters do as they crush juice from the grapes. His cry of judgment will reach the ends of the earth, for the Lord will bring his case against all the nations* (Jeremiah 25:30). Coincidence? Maybe but interesting nevertheless!

ports of meteor sightings are coming into the AMS by the thousands"! *"And there will be strange signs in the sun, moon and stars"* (Luke 21:25a).

Lately there has been a lot of talk and speculation about the four blood moons and a total solar eclipse happening in 2014 and 2015. These certainly hold some significance, especially since they occur on Jewish feast days. *"The sun shall be turned into darkness, and the moon into blood, before the coming of the great and awesome day of the Lord"* (Joel 2:31; Acts 2:20). These phenomena definitely can take place before the Tribulation (the day of the Lord), although I believe the blood moon and solar eclipse mentioned in Revelation 6:12 are supernatural events heralding the beginning of the Great Tribulation, that is, the final three-and-a-half years.

WARS AND RUMORS OF WARS

We all seem to know what constitutes a war, although that has even changed with the war on terror. As Jesus said, *"For nation shall rise against nation, and kingdom against kingdom"* (Mark 13:7). We have seen world wars, civil wars, tribal warfare, ethnic cleansing, gang wars, military posturing, genocide, drug wars, revolutionary wars, religious wars, and the dreaded war on terror with most of the civilized world fighting Islamo-fascism. Similar to the Nazis, the Islamic State (formerly known as ISIS) aims to conquer the world by killing every person who doesn't believe as they do—anyone who stands in the way of their global caliphate. Interestingly, President Barack Obama refers to the Islamic State as ISIL, which stands for Islamic State of Iraq and the Levant. The Levant encompasses an area that includes Israel—God's Promised Land! He has even stated that the Islamic State is neither Islamic nor a state. O-k-a-y; not sure what his ulterior motive or message is with that assertion. I'll leave that up to you to connect the dots.

Defense Secretary Chuck Hagel told reporters at the Pentagon in August 2014 that the Islamic State was "beyond anything we've seen." General Martin Dempsey, chairman of the US Joint Chiefs of Staff, said, "This is an organization that has an apocalyptic, end-of-days strategic vision and which will eventually have to be defeated."

After World War II, the Cold War wasn't an actual war but just a threat of war (rumor?) and a rise of tensions between the Soviet Union and the Western world that had school children hiding under their desks in preparation for the dreaded sirens that would herald an atomic attack. As of April 2014, according to Wikipedia, the number of ongoing wars in the world is forty-three. Is World War III around the corner?

Countries, nations, ethnic groups, and ideologies are on edge, some of them with their fingers on the red button threatening to initiate a nuclear attack. Will North Korea attack South Korea or won't they? Iran intimidates Israel and Israel says it will retaliate. Or maybe it's the other way around! Rumors of war—yes! (Many rumors may be past that stage by the time you read this.) The world is nearing midnight on the Doomsday clock. We're a long way from sticks and stones, cannons and arrows, rifles and swords. The arsenal now includes biological, chemical, and nuclear weapons, with crazies who aren't afraid to use them.

REBELLION AND REVOLUTION

Rebellion has been around since the Garden of Eden but became a more recent phenomenon with the so-called Arab Spring and accompanying revolutions around the world. Their goal is to depose leaders and cause chaos. Millions of angry protestors have taken to the streets in uprisings against their governments. It started in November 2010 with massive demonstrations in Tunisia, followed by the fall of Mubarak in Egypt, Hussein in Iraq, Ghaddafi in Libya, with civil uprisings in Bahrain, Yemen, Lebanon, Algeria, Morocco, Jordan, Iran, and Syria. The citizens say they want democracy, but Islamists have filled the vacuum of many now-leaderless Middle Eastern countries.

Egypt has been torn in two between the Islamists (formerly the Muslim Brotherhood) and the military leaders with both groups claiming victory. The people really don't know which of these two groups are out for their best interests so they riot against each and every faction that comes into power. *"I will make Egyptians fight against each other—brother against brother, neighbor against neighbor, city against city, province against province. The Egyptians will lose heart and I will confuse their plans"* (Isaiah 19:2–3).

With the world's financial situations growing increasingly serious, many European countries have been forced to take severe austerity measures to save their economies. Well, the people don't want to make any personal sacrifices and have taken to the streets to rebel cuts in pensions and social services, the high cost of goods, lower pay, and increased regulations. Riots have broken out in almost every country. There's even a website called *worldatprotest.com* that tracks protests, demonstrations, rallies, and uprisings worldwide!

The Occupy Wall Street movement began in the United States as a protest against government bailouts of the banks and large corporations, and what is perceived to be the rich getting richer to the detriment of the poor and middle class. Since they don't have a coherent message, the Occupiers rail against anything and everything. Americans are incredibly spoiled by their God-given blessings of the past and a sense of entitlement has destroyed the morals, hard work ethic, and perseverance of many. Most young people today are way too angry, moody, lazy, and rebellious, leaning towards total anarchy and scaring the wits out of us older folks. My daughter was working a pony ring when a five-year-old boy was put on a lovely pony. His face was all scrunched up into a frown. My daughter asked him, "What's wrong? It's a beautiful day and you're on a lovely little pony!" He screamed, "I'm angry!" This was a five-year-old! On a pony! But I digress.

Social networking has contributed to these revolutions as instant communication alerts those to meet on a certain day, in a certain place. It doesn't take long for large crowds to throng a public square or park. So many malcontents, so little humility.

When the innocent verdict was read in the Michael Brown case—a black youth who was killed by a white police officer—race riots broke out in Ferguson, Missouri, as well as across the country. Looting, fires, and protesting galore. I saw a sign reading, "Only Revolution Can Bring Justice." Many of the held-high placards were representative of the International Socialist Organization, Peoples Power Assembly, and CUNY International Club.

The culture of government dependency is so ingrained into today's society that if a Great Depression were to occur again, martial law would need to be declared. People do not know how to care for themselves anymore. After Hurricane Katrina, the residents of New Orleans were incapable of providing for themselves and were totally dependent on the government for food, clothing, and shelter. Governments are becoming incapable of fulfilling promises for food stamps, pensions, health care, etc. Society expects good things to be handed to them for just being alive!

Most of all, the peoples of the world are all looking for a hero. Hmm, seems the time is ripe for the rise of the Antichrist to fill the leadership void. If you're reading this during the Tribulation, he may already be in power.

They refused to obey and they were not mindful of Your wonders that You did among them. But they hardened their necks and in their rebellion, they appointed a leader, to return to their bondage (Nehemiah 9:17).

GLOBALIZATION

Unity at all costs has become a reality and a necessary piece-of-the-puzzle for the last days. Under the reign of Antichrist, there will be one religion, one economy, and one government. This has been the dream of society since the Tower of Babel—the belief that there would be no need for war if we all lived as one. Songs such as "We are the World" and "Imagine" espouse how wonderful it would be if there weren't any nations or religions, or anything to separate us. But God stopped the construction of the Tower of Babel and scattered the people by giving them different languages. Frankly, I believe that people prefer to be with their own kind, and that's not a bad thing.

Ecumenism is attempting to bring all religions together. There's even a bumper sticker with the word COEXIST created from different religious symbols. Yes, Jesus taught us to love one another and witness to the lost; however, Christians and Jews are to be set apart and not live like/with the heathen. *"Do not be unequally yoked together with unbelievers. For what fellowship has righteousness with lawlessness? And what communion has light with darkness?" …Therefore, "Come out from among them and be separate," says the Lord. "Do not touch what is unclean, and I will receive you"* (2 Corinthians 6:14,17). The bringing together of all religions is a giant step toward putting the New World Order in place during the Tribulation.

Today, we have a global economy with international trade, jobs being outsourced to foreign countries, and capital and investment movements. What happens to the stock market on one side of the world affects the other side. We have the World Trade Organization, the International Monetary Fund, and the World Bank. They seek to distribute the wealth of the world from richer countries to poorer countries in an effort to eliminate poverty and create economic parity, ultimately creating a global currency.

The United Nations is an international organization founded in 1945 and based in New York City in order to maintain international peace and security, promote social progress and human rights, and become a clearing-house for nations to communicate. However, in their efforts to solve the world's problems, they have become somewhat of a monster. Their Agenda 21 seeks to move the world's populations into cities or "settlement zones" (to more easily control the population?!) and eliminate family farms and private property on behalf of "earth sustainability." This action plan can only lead to social engineering and communism through population reduction and control. Agenda 21 is another plan of action towards the New World Order.

The New World Order refers to a new period of history with dramatic changes in global political thoughts and balances of power towards a one-world government, one-world economy, and one-world religion. Groups like the Freemasons, Bilderberg Group, Trilateral Commission, and Illuminati control the flow of events from behind the scenes—a shadow government—nudging us covertly and continuously in the direction of a world government for the Antichrist. *And all the world marveled and followed the beast* (Revelation 13:3b).

UNESCO (United Nations Educational, Scientific and Cultural Organization) has a plan to indoctrinate children with a global agenda, since adults are more savvy and thus, suspicious of their goals. Hitler went after the youth; Obama went after the youth; Muslims went after the youth. A generation of children has been swayed through the public school system, taught to value globalization, environmentalism, and social justice over personal responsibility and free enterprise. Our kids have been brainwashed—no more prayer, no more Christmas, no more patriotism. Oh, but they hold celebrations for Earth Day!

The material my children brought home when they were in public school shocked me. They were told to keep private journals of their home life and their feelings, which the teachers graded. Oh, but they instructed the kids not to show their parents. (Of course, mine did!) A new rule in our local school system strips children of their individuality by forbidding them to wear shirts with any kind of words or symbols. There is some serious indoctrination towards a New World Order going on in the public school system, from pre-kindergarten through the university level.

The militarization of our police force is getting worrisome. SWAT teams barge into homes with no proof of wrongdoing inside. Law enforcement is asking for identification from random people on the street. In November 2013, drivers along a busy Fort Worth, Texas, street were stopped at a police roadblock and directed into a parking lot, where they were asked by federal contractors for samples of their breath, saliva, and even blood. This is how it starts—and ends badly.

Little by little, first this and then that, lower expectations and remove national pride, take away specialness, a minor adjustment here, make everyone feel the same. Before you know it, people can't think for themselves, and these little intrusions become the normal way of life.

Global government is gaining traction as well. In 2002, the African Union was created with its own flag and consisting of fifty-four states (all except Morocco). A Mediterranean Union is also in the works. The European Union's goal is the dissolving of nations to become a tyrannical superpower and elect a super-president!

Global Future 2045 is a group of the world's leading scientists, technologists, spiritual leaders, futurists, and philosophers who believe "the world stands on the threshold of global change." It is premised on the notion that in order for civilization to move to a higher stage of development, humanity needs a scientific revolution along with significant spiritual changes that will be inseparably linked.

I've lived in America all of my life, and I never thought I would see the day when this great superpower, which was abundantly blessed by God, would turn evil and be diminished on the world stage. Our leaders deliberately brought us down. I always wondered why the United States was never mentioned in Bible prophecy since it was such a huge player in the re-creation of Israel and the most powerful nation in the world. Not anymore! It needed to happen to bring us closer to the NWO.

PERSECUTION

God's people face opposition daily even now and persecution against Jews and Christians intensifies during the Tribulation. *"You will be hated all over the world because of your allegiance to me"* (Matthew 24:9 NLT). This, too, is nothing new because Satan hates the children of God. The Jewish people have tasted Egyptian slavery and the Holocaust. They are called dirty names; their small businesses are vandalized. Anti-Semitism is spreading while the Muslim world swears to wipe Israel off the map.

The attacks against Christians started almost immediately with all apostles, except John, being horribly killed. The early Roman Empire was especially brutal as Christians were thrown to the lions for sport or their decapitated heads set on fire and used as lampposts by Nero. Since then, untold numbers of missionaries have been martyred, and continue to be. Persecution against Christians today is especially bad in the ever-growing Islamic countries, as well as communist China, North Korea, and socialist Latin countries. According to The Pew Research Center, *The Economist,* Christians today are the most persecuted religious group in the world. Even Europe has become atheistic and agnostic and is increasingly hostile to the Gospel. Beautiful cathedrals are now museums, or worse, mosques.

Globalists think Christians stand in their way of Utopia, and too many college professors teach that Christians are naïve and stupid. Actually, it is the professors who are blind and foolish. *Professing to be wise, they became fools* (Romans 1:22).

And in America, with its strong Judeo-Christian roots, Christians are now ridiculed, ignored, or misunderstood. A high-school girl was confronted by a classmate holding a gun on her with the question, "Do you believe in God?" Cassie affirmed, "Yes!" and became a contemporary martyr.

Wonderful childhood memories of Christmas are now only that because public displays cannot even mention Jesus. There is actually a war on Christmas! Christians are called "intolerant" or "bigots" and our freedom of speech is threatened. Prayer has essentially been removed from our public schools and the Ten Commandments from our courtrooms. And we know it will only get worse as the Muslim population grows and a post-modern, post-Christian society grows alongside it, in Satan's attempt to yet again destroy the people of the true God.

TECHNOLOGICAL ADVANCEMENTS

One of the most obvious signs that we're living in the very last days is how technologically advanced our world has become. A telling and astonishing verse appears in the Old Testament prophets, *But you, Daniel, keep this prophecy a secret until the time of the end. Many will travel to and fro, and knowledge will increase* (Daniel 12:4 NLT).

From the beginning of mankind until the mid-1800s, there were no automobiles, televisions, airplanes, computers, electricity, plastic, refrigeration, light bulbs, indoor plumbing, and a whole bunch of other inventions. In my own lifetime, we've gone from not having air conditioning to the International Space Station! From computers that took up an entire room to ones that can fit on a fingertip. My kids can hardly believe it when I tell them that we didn't have cell phones, color televisions, video games, the Internet, DVDs, microwave ovens, digital cameras, iPods/iPads, global positioning systems, or personal computers when I was growing up. We didn't even have ballpoint pens! When I learned how to write, it was with a nib and fountain pen.

Man's intelligence for invention has taken a giant leap forward in a relatively short time period. The modes of transportation just 250 years ago were the horse and buggy or a wooden boat. It wasn't until the Industrial Revolution that man figured out how to build a steam engine for locomotives (which have progressed into the bullet train) or ships (we now have nuclear submarines). The inventions of the automobile and airplane have taken us further, faster, than we could've imagined not that very long ago.

Jetting around the world is normal! Traveling to and fro, indeed.

It can't be denied that knowledge has greatly increased in the field of medicine. CT and MRI scans are only the beginning of diagnostic testing. Tiny cameras in the form of a pill can be swallowed and the results recorded as it moves through the digestive tract. Complex surgeries and new medicines are saving lives every day. Life expectancies are on the rise for those who have access to good health care. Scientists are learning new mysteries of the human body at a rapid pace.

Knowledge and wisdom are tools for good in the hands of the godly; however, this increase in knowledge is also creating proverbial monsters. Cloning, eugenics, and DNA experimentation open up all sorts of ethical issues (does a clone or a chimera have a soul? Will humans have the power to create new races? Or will God stop us before we all get killed?).

We have learned new ways to save human life but, unfortunately, we've also learned new ways to take it as well. Technology has created new weapons that can inflict incredible death and destruction, and for the first time in history, we now have the capability of destroying all life on the earth.

Global communications have brought new light to signs that we are in the last days. During the Tribulation, it is written of the Two Witnesses, *And for three and a half days, all peoples, tribes, languages and nations will come to stare at their* [dead] *bodies* (Revelation 11:9 NLT). Thanks to satellite television, only now can we understand how everyone in the whole world would be able to see the bodies of the Two Witnesses.

Another prophecy that is now able to be fulfilled due to satellites and air travel: *"And the Good News about the Kingdom will be preached throughout the whole world, so that all nations will hear it, and then finally the end will come"* (Matthew 24:14 NLT). This worldwide preaching of the Gospel intensifies during the Tribulation when the proclaiming angel, the Two Witnesses, and the 144,000 Jewish evangelists spread the good news to the world's inhabitants, but more on them later.

A technological advance that has implications for the Tribulation is the electronic delivery of monetary funds, currently with debit cards and electronic funds transfers via smart phones and computers. The cashless society is nearly upon us; it may already be a reality for you. To deter identity theft and other supposed good reasons, a bio-chip inserted under the skin, QR tattoo, or RFID ink will contain complete personal information about us, including our unique identification number for banking, plus a global positioning system for tracking. This sounds all neat and tidy, until it is realized that a dictator could easily take control of this system, finding all dissenters and allowing only certain people to buy or sell. *And no one could buy or sell anything without that mark* (Revelation 13:17 NLT).

When I was a kid, even in the city, there weren't any cameras watching my every move. Surveillance is now taken to extremes with cameras on almost every urban corner, outside every store, and along the roadways. You can't board an airplane without being subjected to invasive scans that see through your clothing. New scanners can even see through buildings! Drones and eye-in-the-sky satellites can see details on the ground. Every time you swipe a debit/credit card, travel with a toll transponder or GPS, or turn on your smart phone, you can be located. E-mails and tweets are saved for possible use against you in a court of law. Facial recognition technology has been collecting faces from every possible source. Satellite payloads used to be announced with pride but are now "secret." What are they hiding? What can they see?

Miniature drones, or micro air vehicles (MAVs), based on the same physics used by flying insects and integrating nano-mimicry, have been deployed. The US Air Force unveiled insect-sized spies that could not be detected and would be able to stealthily fly into buildings and caves to photograph, record, and even attack with little stingers. The University of Pennsylvania's GRASP lab recently showed off drones that swarm, flying in synchronized formations, with little or no direct human supervision. The US military research agency conducted a symposium discussing "bugs, bots, borgs, and bio-weapons." *Then out of the smoke locusts came upon the earth. And to them was given power, as the scorpions of the earth have power* (Revelation 9:3). This probably refers to demonic beings from verse seven; however, they sound suspiciously like these tiny drones.

The US Department of Homeland Security has added underwater drones to their arsenal with robots based on fish movements. Robocod can dart around the water just like a real fish and can access hard-to-reach areas. There is nowhere to hide!

On April 4, 2012, *The Washington Times* reported "Scientists at the Defense Advanced Research Projects Agency are working on ways to create insect cyborgs, by incorporating mechanical elements into larvae and then using them to control the fully grown insect when it emerges." Talk about the proverbial fly on the wall! Big Brother is definitely watching. And listening. Buh-bye privacy.

Technology has now produced the hologram—an image that appears as a real person who can speak, move and, yes, accept worship as the Antichrist demands. It doesn't just appear as a real person but actually is the real person. This is a sign of the times that really clinches it for me that the end is imminent.

At the rate of progress in the last hundred years, I can only imagine what is in store for us as mankind continues to expand his knowledge in these last days.

ISRAEL

If the previous signs are the size of posters, Israel is a billboard. Or skywriting in big loopy letters across a deep blue background. As the people and the land that God has chosen for His very own, the story of the Jews and Israel is an epic spanning from the beginning of history to the present day. Through Israel, God taught the Jews what He expects of humans, and we get to reap the lessons that they had to endure. *These things happened to them for examples, and they were written for our admonition, upon whom the ends of the world are come* (1 Corinthians 10:11). At this time, most Jews still reject Jesus as the Messiah, although that changes in the Tribulation.

In the Bible, the fig tree is sometimes identified as the nation of Israel. (See Judges 9:10, Hosea 9:10, Joel 1:7, Luke 13:6, Matthew 21:19, Jeremiah 24:5.) For centuries, Israel seemed to be a dead tree. *A man planted a fig tree in his garden and came again and again to see if there was any fruit on it but he was always disappointed. Finally he said to his gardener, "Cut it down. It's taking up space we can use for something else." The gardener answered, "Give it one more chance and I'll give it special attention"* (Luke 13:6–8 NLT).

In 70 AD, the Romans destroyed Jerusalem and scattered the Jews in every direction. *For the Lord will scatter you among all the nations, from one end of the earth to the other* (Deuteronomy 28:64–67 NLT). For almost two thousand years, the land of Israel was a desolate wasteland as the *diaspora* had the Jewish people looking for a safe place to settle, dispersed to various countries around the globe. Unique among all other emigrant groups, the Jewish people have kept their identity, ethnicity, language (Hebrew), and religion intact despite intense persecution and prejudice.

God's enemy, Satan, seeks to destroy Israel at every turn but his plans always backfire. In the aftermath of the Holocaust, the Jews received pity and were allowed to return to their homeland. The "dry bones and graves" were resurrected. So it was that on May 14, 1948, Israel became a nation. *"Who has ever seen or heard of anything as strange as this? Has a nation ever been born in a single day? Has a country ever come forth in a mere moment? But by the time Jerusalem's birth pains begin, the baby will be born; the nation will come forth"* (Isaiah 66:8 NLT).

Approximately six million Jews have returned to Israel in recent years. Israel's leaves have sprouted. Increased rainfall and irrigation technology have caused the land to blossom, and they are now able to actually export produce. Tel Aviv is a modern, thriving city, and their military is one of the best in the world. Oil and natural gas have recently been discovered. And they have God actively involved in all of their affairs whether they realize it yet or not. During the Tribulation, Israel is the center of attention for the whole world as Daniel's prophecies regarding their 70th Week unfolds.

The players in the Gog and Magog War mentioned in Ezekiel 38-39 are aligning themselves in the present day. Russia (Magog), Iran (Persia), Sudan (Cush), and Turkey (Mesach) have different motives but are joining militarily to defeat Israel. The nations of the world are putting political pressure on the tiny country to surrender land and divide Jerusalem.

There is an interesting prophecy that has freaked me out lately. Leaders all around the world are calling for a two-state solution to the Israel-Palestinian problem, stating that it is in the interest of "peace and security" or "peace and safety." Almost every world leader has uttered that phrase. In a speech on December 3, 2014 at Georgetown University, Hilary Clinton said, "Smart power is using every possible tool and partner to advance peace and security." Well, get this: *For when they say, "Peace and safety!" then sudden destruction comes upon them, as labor pains upon a pregnant woman. And they shall not escape* (1 Thessalonians 5:3). Note: The ESV (English Standard Version) uses the actual words "peace and security" in this verse.

There are non-biblical prophecies that are aligning as well. Nostradamus predicted a catastrophic world war occurring in the early twenty-first century and Muslims are awaiting the Mahdi, the Twelfth Imam, who sounds like he could be the Antichrist. In the Rue de Bac, Paris, France in July 1830, an apparition of Mary said, "There will be bad times to come…The whole world will be turned upside-down by misfortunes of all kinds." In *The Prophecy of the Popes*, St. Malachy described the succession of Roman Catholic popes, which have been somewhat accurate with Pope Benedict the next-to-last and Pope Francis a hiccup before the last Pope Peter the Roman. We are not to set dates or put stock in these extra-biblical sources, but we are to discern the signs of the times. World events are following the birth pang timelines that Jesus gave us as a warning of His soon return.

I recently heard a cute and insightful story about a missionary in a primitive tribal village. One day, a group of women asked the missionary, "Are the leaves almost finished?" The missionary was perplexed about what they were trying to ask until they gestured for his Bible. Their spokeswoman asked, "Where is Adam?" and he went to the beginning of the book. "Where is Moses?" and he went forward a few pages. "Where is David?" as he moved forward. "Where is Jesus?" and he riffled the pages forward to the New Testament. "And where are we?" The missionary paused before turning any pages. Hmm, we're not in the book of Acts and we're not yet in Revelation, so he indicated the section including the epistles and said, "We're somewhere in here." Excitedly, the woman exclaimed, "It's true! The leaves are nearly finished!" This is an interesting way they viewed the Bible as a timeline for the history of humankind.

Future events cast their shadows before them and the events that will be full-blown during the Tribulation are manifesting themselves in lesser ways even now. The signs are here for us to observe, and it is the will of God that we are aware of them and so are able to discern the times. It's been said, to those who refuse to believe, no amount of proof is sufficient, and to those who do believe, no proof is necessary. I believe wholeheartedly, and I'm hoping the signs of the times will prove to you that the hour is, indeed, late.

The signs are all around us, impossible to ignore. And the sign of His Second Coming—Act One is the final wake-up call for the world as the Rapture resolves all doubt that the Tribulation is at hand.

Chapter 4
THE RAPTURE

*And love just like that will bring Him back for
the few He can call His friends.*

KEITH GREEN

The Rapture is an event so catastrophic that it will change the world, ushering in the New World Order and the empire of the Antichrist. If you're reading this during the Tribulation, then the Rapture has already happened!

The term, Rapture, comes from the Latin word *rapio* or *rapere* and the Greek word *harpazo,* which means to catch up, to snatch away, or to take out. *For the Lord Himself will descend from heaven with a shout, with the voice of an archangel, and with the trumpet of God. And the dead in Christ will rise first. Then we who are alive and remain shall be caught up together [harpazo] with them in the clouds to meet the Lord in the air. And thus we shall always be with the Lord. Therefore comfort one another with these words* (1 Thessalonians 4:16-1).

It is described as a mystery, something that is unusual, a secret. *We speak of God's secret wisdom, a wisdom that has been hidden and that God destined for our glory before time began. None of the rulers of this age understood it, for if they had, they would not have crucified the Lord of glory* (1 Corinthians 2:7–8 NLT). Paul is saying that if Satan and his minions understood the extent of the blessings God had planned for the Church, including the Rapture, they would have done everything possible to prevent the crucifixion. Satan knows plenty but he doesn't know everything, and it's always best to keep your enemy guessing!

Jesus is now in heaven preparing a place for us. *"And if I go and prepare a place for you, I will come again and receive you to Myself; that where I am, there you may be also"* (John 14:3). I can hardly imagine the landscaping and interior decorating that's been going on!

Our mortal bodies are not fit for heaven so believers who have lived during the approximately two-thousand-year Age of Grace receive their immortal, glorified bodies at the Rapture. *Behold, I tell you a mystery; we shall not all sleep but we shall be changed, in a moment, in the twinkling of an eye, at the last trumpet* (1 Corinthians 15:51–52). *He will take these weak mortal bodies of ours and change them into glorious bodies like his own, using the same mighty power that he will use to conquer everything, everywhere* (Philippians 3:21 NLT).

> What are resurrected bodies like? We get clues by looking at the resurrected body of Jesus. He (1) looked like a human; (2) ate food; (3) was physical and not a ghost; (4) was recognizable; (5) retained his personality; (6) moved through solid walls and appeared at will; and (7) apparently looked to be about 30 years old.

There are disagreements about whether all children go in the Rapture. The *Left Behind* series by Tim LaHaye and Jerry Jenkins assumes that they do. It may appeal to our emotions that little babies are so innocent and good. However, we are born with "original sin"—we are not born innocent. I've seen some evil two-year-olds! Also, in the Old Testament, God commanded the Israelites to slay children right along with the others who got in the way of the Promised Land. They didn't receive any special treatment. I do believe that some children go in the Rapture, even before the so-called "age of reason." It's biblical that in many cases, a saved person's close family or household gets saved as well. *Only Rahab the harlot shall live, she and all who are with her in the house, because she hid the messengers that we sent* (Joseph 6:17). God showed mercy to Rahab's entire household on account of her righteousness. But ultimately, I believe that God knows all who would accept Him.

The Rapture has a global impact instigating untold catastrophes as driverless cars and airplanes crash, riots break out in prisons as guards disappear, doctors and nurses abandon their patients in the middle of surgery, factory workers are no longer on the assembly line to produce goods, and absent government officials cause a gap in leadership. People are in a panic. Fear grips every town, every city, every country. Apostate Christians who thought they were going to heaven get a rude awakening when they realize that they've been left behind.

The media quickly looks for answers to report the sudden disappearance of millions of people, interviewing every so-called expert on the subject. But, of course, all of the real experts are no longer around to ask. I can only guess at what explanation is given. Esoteric authors suggest that the "unenlightened" must be removed before the New Age can begin. Some say that aliens took us, or maybe a time warp, a dimension shift, or a new weapon of mass destruction. Satan knows that his plan for world domination would be over in a heartbeat if everyone knew the real story of what happened to all those people.

Those who are left behind will be susceptible to believing the lie. People harden their hearts and, in fear, look for a leader who can save them, opening the door for the Antichrist. God sends this great delusion to the minds of the unbelievers, and with the Holy Spirit (residing inside Christians) taken out of the world, evil has full reign.

TIMING OF THE RAPTURE

Every Christian believes in the Second Coming of Christ; however, it is the timing of the Rapture that has been debated. In my forty years of study and prayer, I am convinced that it happens before the Tribulation.

Christ's Second Coming consists of two acts—(1) when Jesus returns for His own in the sky in the event referred to as the Rapture; and (2) when Jesus returns to the earth to conquer, rule, and reign. The very purpose of the Tribulation excludes the whole issue of grace. Jesus promises to deliver believers from the "hour of trial" that is coming upon the earth. *"Because you have obeyed my command to persevere, I will keep you from the great time of testing that will come upon the whole world"* (Revelation 3:10 NLT). *He is the one who has rescued us from the terrors of the coming judgment* (1 Thessalonians 1:10 NLT). *For God decided to save us through our Lord Jesus Christ, not to pour out His anger on us* (1 Thessalonians 5:9 NLT).

"They will be my people," says the Almighty. *"On the day when I act, they will be My own special treasure. I will spare them as a father spares an obedient*

and dutiful child" (Malachi 3:17 NLT). *Come my people, enter your chambers, and shut your doors behind you. Hide yourself, as it were, for a little moment. Until the indignation is past* (Isaiah 26:20).

We are repeatedly reminded to watch for the appearing of the Lord, to *"be ready"* (Matthew 24:44), *"to be dressed in readiness and keep our lamps lit"* (Luke 12:35). We are told to always be ready because He comes like a thief in the night to those who aren't watching. *"If therefore you will not watch, I will come on you like a thief and you will not know what hour I will come"* (Revelation 3:3 NLT).

Matthew 24 is an important chapter regarding the end times; however, Jesus is answering more than one question that the disciples pose, so the timing isn't always clear. For instance, the verse *"Then two men will be working in a field: one will be taken and the other left. Two women will be grinding: one will be taken and the other left. Watch therefore for you do not know what hour your Lord is coming"* (Matthew 24:40–42) can be speaking about the Rapture as well as the Second Coming. Many prophecies have dual meanings—one for the times in which they were written and one that looks forward to a future fulfillment. Since Jesus is speaking to His Jewish disciples here, I believe that ultimately this chapter concerns Israel.

Whether speaking about the Rapture or the Second Coming, it is true that we do not know the day or the hour, but we are to know the season or the times. Those with a personal relationship with Jesus may very well discern when the Rapture is about to happen, and as I write this, the Spirit is telling me it is very soon. *But you aren't in the dark about these things dear brothers and sisters, and you won't be surprised when the day of the Lord comes like a thief. For you are all children of the light and of the day; we don't belong to darkness and night. So be on your guard, not asleep like the others* (1 Thessalonians 5:4–6 NLT).

"When the Son of Man returns, the world will be like the people were in Noah's day. In those days before the flood, the people enjoyed banquets and parties and weddings right up to the time Noah entered his boat and the flood came to destroy them all" (Luke 17:26–27 NLT). The world will be in such terrible turmoil that it seems unlikely He is referring to after the Tribulation. I don't think there will be much partying going on then, so Act 1 of Jesus' return must happen before the Tribulation.

Those who believe that the Rapture happens after the Tribulation have to reconcile that Jesus comes down and then goes right up and then comes down. That would be almost ridiculous. There also needs to be live, believing survivors to populate the Millennial Kingdom.

In the beginning of the book of Revelation, Jesus gives seven messages to the Church followed by a trumpet blast and the words, *"Come up here and I will show you what must happen after these things"* (Revelation 4:1). John then sees twenty-four elders seated on thrones around Christ's, which corresponds to the verse, *For he raised us from the dead along with Christ, and we are seated with him in the heavenly realm* (Ephesians 2:6 NLT). So in Revelation 5, the Church on the earth is caught up to heaven and isn't mentioned again until Revelation 19—after the Tribulation verses about the judgments. *"When everything is ready, I will come and get you so that you will always be where I am"* (John 14:3 NLT).

God sent angels to physically remove Lot and his family from Sodom before it could be destroyed, along with the admonition to "not look back." *When Lot still hesitated, the angels seized his hand and the hands of his wife and two daughters and rushed them safely outside the city, for the Lord was merciful* (Genesis 19:16 NLT).

Just as there were three kinds of people on the earth at the time of the Great Flood, there are three kinds of people at the end of days: the unbelievers who perished in the Flood (Tribulation); Noah and his family (Jews and new saints) who went through it; and Enoch (Church) who was taken to heaven before it. According to Hebrew tradition, Enoch was born on the day that would become Pentecost, the day the Church was "born." Enoch is a type of the Church and his disappearance before the Flood gives us a hint of a pre-tribulation Rapture. The Church must be off the earth during this time because Jesus already paid our judgment, and if we have believed without seeing are thereby rewarded with the Rapture.

Since the Tribulation is God's dispensation to complete His promise to the Jewish people and focus on Israel, there is no need for the Church to be on Earth. It is during the Tribulation when the Jews recognize that Jesus is their Messiah. I believe that it cannot begin until the Church is gone from the earth in the Rapture. It is an event without any prerequisite events, and in fact, appears to trigger the setup for the Tribulation due to its chaotic shock to the whole world. There may be a time gap to accomplish the rebuilding of the Temple and Babylon (if this is spoken of literally), the awakening of the Jews, the rise of Antichrist, and allow certain technologies to be in place.

The Parable of the Fig Tree is another clue to the timing of the Rapture and the last days. *"Now learn a lesson from the fig tree. When its branches bud and its leaves begin to sprout, you know that summer is near. In the same way, when you see all these things, you can know his return is very near, right at the door. I tell you the truth; this generation will not pass from the scene until all these things take place"* (Matthew 24:32–34 NLT). Some commentators say that the word "generation" here should be translated "race" or "age." Those two words have different meanings and if God meant something else, He would've said it! But He used the word "generation," just as it's used in other verses meaning just that.

Ever since I first read this verse, I felt in my heart that my generation would be the last generation before Jesus returned. *The days of our lives are seventy years; and if by reason of strength they are eighty years* (Psalm 90:10). So those who were alive when Israel became a nation in 1948 (the budding fig tree—see 1 Kings 4:25; Hosea 9:10), and have seen all the signs spoken of in the previous chapter, would still be alive at the Second Coming, which comes after the Tribulation, which comes after the Rapture. Well, I'm getting excited just thinking how close it all could be!

God's thoughts are not ours, and the Rapture is called a mystery. Sometimes confusion arises regarding the meaning of certain terms, such as the last trumpet, the last day, the fig tree, and whether or not vultures can be translated as eagles. However, God's promises to His Church make it clear that the bride will escape the wrath, while God's Word to Tribulation saints is that most will lose their lives. *And the beast was allowed to wage war against God's holy people and to overcome them* (Revelation 13:7 NLT).

REASONS FOR THE RAPTURE

One of the reasons that the Rapture needs to happen is to take up God's people before all hell breaks loose. Just as countries recall their ambassadors before war is declared, so too, Jesus takes His ambassadors home before He unleashes judgment. If I were to fumigate my house for termites, I would make sure my children and pets were removed before the toxic chemicals went in. By faith and grace, a Christian's sin has been covered by the blood that Jesus shed on the cross and, thus, has been declared righteous. No condemnation equals no wrath.

In heaven, there needs to be sufficient time (seven years?) to review our lives and receive our rewards at the Bema Seat judgment, which is followed by the Marriage Ceremony before returning victorious with Jesus at the Battle of Armageddon. (I believe the actual Marriage Supper of the Lamb occurs at the start of the Millennium to accommodate the Tribulation and Old Testament saints, and the guests who survived the Tribulation.)

The Rapture is also a reward for those who, during the Church Age, believed by faith only and not due to God exhibiting big displays of power. *We live by faith and not by sight* (2 Corinthians 5:7). In the Old Testament, acts of God include the burning bush, the Egyptian plagues, manna, fire and brimstone, pillars of clouds and fire, the parting of the Red Sea, the Flood, the lions' den, Balaam's donkey, Jonah's whale, Jericho's walls, and more. The advent of Jesus Christ brought the Star of Bethlehem, miracles of healing, deliverance, commanding nature, and a big one—the Resurrection. However, since the Holy Spirit arrived at Pentecost, God has been working behind the scenes in and through His people. Still working miracles but on a smaller, more intimate scale. Those who have passed this test of faith, who have believed in God even without seeing Him, are special in God's eyes and will be rewarded with that Blessed Hope, the Rapture. *"Blessed are those who have not seen and yet have believed"* (John 20:29). Which is why I believe that the Gog and Magog War occurs after the Rapture, because God will display His power.

Another important reason for the Rapture is to shake up the heathen and wake up the Jews. God doesn't want anyone to perish, and this event leaves a big impression on the world and sets the stage for the final implementation of the New World Order. The Rapture pushes the "pause" button while God focuses on Israel.

"Seventy weeks are determined for your people and for your holy city, to finish

the transgression, to make an end of sins, to make reconciliation for iniquity, to bring in everlasting righteousness, to seal up the vision and prophecy, and to anoint the Most Holy. Know therefore and understand, that from the going forth of the command to restore and to build Jerusalem until Messiah the Prince there shall be seven weeks, and sixty-two weeks: the street shall be built again, and the wall, even in troublesome times" (Daniel 9:24–25).

The seventy weeks are actually seventy "weeks" of years, or 490 years. Five hundred years before Christ, Daniel predicted that 483 years would pass between the time a decree was made to rebuild Jerusalem and the time when the Messiah would die. Historians tell us that, using the 360-day calendar, 483 years (173,880 days) passed from March 14, 445 BC to April 6, 32 AD; between the time Artaxerxes issued the decree until Jesus' ride into Jerusalem on a donkey. According to Daniels' timetable, there are seven missing years—the clock stopped ticking during the Church age and starts again after the Rapture.

CLUES IN THE JEWISH FEASTS

"These are the set times of the LORD, the sacred occasions, which you shall celebrate each at its appointed time" (Leviticus 23:4).

Leviticus 23 sums up God's eternal plan, ingeniously revealed through the timing and nature of the seven annual Feasts of the Lord. The seven feasts and their dates on the Hebrew calendar are:

1. Passover (Pesach) – Nisan 14–15
2. Unleavened Bread (Chag Hamotzi) – Nisan 15–22
3. First Fruits (Yom hamikkurim) – Nisan 16–17
4. Pentecost (Shavuot) – Sivan 6–7
5. Trumpets (Rosh Hoshanah) – Tishri 1
6. Atonement (Yom Kippur) – Tishri 10
7. Tabernacles (Sukkot) – Tishri 15–22

The amazing thing is how these Jewish feast days were fulfilled, or will be fulfilled, by Jesus. The first four are considered the spring feasts and have already happened.

1. Passover = Jesus' death as the sacrificial lamb.
2. Unleavened Bread = Jesus' burial. Leaven symbolizes sin, and the body of Jesus, who is the Bread of Life, was without sin.
3. Firstfruits = Jesus' resurrection. *But now Christ is risen from the dead, and has become the firstfruits of those who have fallen asleep* (1 Corinthians 15:20).
4. Pentecost = the Church when the Holy Spirit indwelt believers as Jesus promised. This event occurred fifty days after the Firstfruits, as it does in the Jewish feast.
5. Trumpets = the Rapture. This feast occurs in the fall, after a period of time seeming to represent the Church Age. The trumpet was the signal for the field workers to come into the Temple. This feast day also represents the beginning of the Jewish new year corresponding to the creation of humans.
6. Atonement = the Tribulation, when the world will atone for its sins, culminating in the Second Coming.
7. Tabernacles = the Millennial Kingdom, when Jesus lives or "tabernacles" with us.

There are other Jewish feasts that give us insight into the mystery of the Rapture. In a Jewish wedding, a man would write a marriage covenant, which he would then present to the intended bride and her father. She indicated her acceptance to the proposal by taking a cup of wine from him. With this betrothal, the groom negotiated a fair price for his bride. (Believers have been bought with the Lord's sacrificial blood.) Then the husband-to-be would leave with the announcement, "I'm going to prepare a place for you, and I'll return when it's ready." This separation/engagement period usually lasted about a year while the groom constructed a place for them to live at or near his father's house. The groom's father had to deem their new home ready, and so if asked the date of the wedding, the groom would reply, "Only my father knows." (See Matthew 24:36.) Meanwhile, the bride would make herself beautiful, keeping a lamp (Holy Spirit) and her wedding clothes (righteousness through Christ) beside her bed, accumulating her trousseau (our righteous acts) because she wasn't sure exactly what day her groom would come for her. (See Matthew 25:1–12.) When all was ready, the groom and his friends approached the bride's house; they would shout and blow a shofar to announce their readiness. (See 1 Corinthians 15:52.) Once the bride was "fetched" (Rapture), the two would return to the father's house where they were secluded in a bridal chamber to consummate their marriage; the honeymoon would last for seven nights (seven-year tribulation?). After the honeymoon, the newlyweds emerge to greet their guests and celebrate at a great feast (the Marriage Supper of the Lamb).

There's never a dull moment when you consider the ways of God! Check out the stories of Ruth and Boaz, Daniel's friends in the oven, Isaac's sacrifice, the destruction of Jericho, the parables of the wedding banquet, and the ten bridesmaids for more clues about the Rapture.

Because I mention the Rapture so frequently, I have been accused by my friends and family to be an escapist. Well, yeah! Between the struggles to make a living and trying to get through this life in one piece, who wouldn't want to escape this dirty world to be with the Lord? Maybe those who have the Mercedes, the big bank account, glowing health, and everything else going for them are happy here. But we know those are all temporary and illusions. So, call me an escapist if you want—I don't mind.

The Rapture may be the greatest evangelistic event of all time as millions of people who have heard about it but never responded realize they've been left behind. They remember something a Christian once said and, if they haven't succumbed to the great delusion, will seek out information. If they believe, they will be saved. And if the Rapture hasn't happened yet, now is the time to preach the Gospel with all urgency to save more souls before the terrible times of the Tribulation arrive.

Therefore comfort each other and edify one another (1 Thessalonians 5:11).

Chapter 5
THE TRIBULATION

The darker the night, the nearer the dawn.

R.A. TORREY

T hat period of horror, which the prophets and Jesus predicted would occur at the end of the world as we know it, is referred to as the Tribulation. Not just your ordinary trouble with a lower case "t" but a unique, all-encompassing trouble that deserves a capital "T."

The Tribulation is referred to as "The Day of the Lord" (Isaiah 2:12, Joel 1:15); "the time of Jacob's trouble" (Jeremiah 30:7); "the day of trouble" (Zephaniah 1:15); "the Great Tribulation" (Matthew 24:21). The adjective "great" is a distinction reserved for the second half of the seven-year time frame.

"For then there will be great tribulation such as has not been since the beginning of the world to this time, no, nor ever shall be" (Matthew 24:21).

From my vantage point, it can be difficult to determine the exact chronology of events, especially with our limited human view. *"For My thoughts are not your thoughts, nor are your ways My ways," says the Lord* (Isaiah 55:8).

Imagine a parade route on a clear summer day. Standing on the side of the street, you watch the parade go by, one marching band or float at a time, craning your neck for a better view. But God, above it all in more ways than one, can see the grand marshal leading the parade *and* the clown holding up the rear, at the same time. He sees the tuba player suffering through the flu, the baton twirler hoping her crush notices her, the toddler with the cotton candy, the policeman tired of working double shifts, and the beauty queen waving to the crowd who worries about aging behind her fake smile—all at the same time. He sees the Big Picture. He knows how it began and how it all ends. And exactly what is going on right now in your life.

The Age of Grace ends when the Church is taken to heaven in the Rapture. The Tribulation officially begins when the Antichrist signs a peace treaty with Israel. Whether immediately or after a short gap, Daniel's missing seventieth week (described in the previous chapter) commences and God once again focuses on Israel.

Because God, the Holy Spirit as He indwells believers, is the only "good" in the world, and having departed at the Rapture, I can only imagine the horrors that mankind inflicts without His restraining influence. *For the mystery of lawlessness is already at work; only He who now restrains will do so until He is taken out of the way* (2 Thessalonians 2:7).

Since the Fall, mankind has determined to do what is right in his own eyes and will be only too happy to be rid of the "goody-goody" Christians. Criminals are emboldened, chaos and looting reigns, rebellion against God rises to a fever pitch—until the Antichrist arrives on the scene to "save the world." Most of the details of what we know about the Tribulation are in the last book of the Bible. *The Revelation of Jesus Christ, which God gave Him to show His servants—things which must shortly take place* (Revelation 1:1).

PURPOSES OF THE TRIBULATION

God uses the Tribulation period to accomplish three primary purposes: (1) to fulfill promises made to Israel; (2) to give every human being a last chance to make their choice; and (3) to mete out judgment and wrath on an unbelieving world. Daniel's missing seven years means that Israel gets to complete its history and see the promises of God fulfilled after many, many years of waiting. Strange things are afoot in Zion as God again concerns Himself with the Jewish people.

The Tribulation is necessary to force the earth's population to make their choice. Is it going to be the Antichrist or Jesus Christ? Time is running out for people who remain on the fence regarding their decision about God. With the intense persecution, natural catastrophes, supernatural occurrences, and especially the mark of the beast, everyone gets the chance to seal their fate. Do you accept or reject God? Will you worship the Antichrist to save your life only to lose your eternal soul? There will be two kinds of people during the Tribulation: those who are looking forward to

Jesus' Glorious Appearing, accepting Him as Savior and showing kindness to the Jews; or they will oppose Christ and join with the Antichrist, accepting his mark to buy and sell and persecuting the Jews. The former who survive will go into the Millennial Kingdom; the latter will be judged and rejected by Christ.

Not only do the Jews return to the Lord, but many Tribulation saints also find salvation—although, the majority are beheaded for their faith. *Then I saw the souls of those who had been beheaded for their witness to Jesus and for the word of God, who had not worshiped the beast or his image, and had not received his mark on their foreheads or on their hands* (Revelation 20:4).

Another purpose for the Tribulation is so God can pour out His righteous judgment on an unbelieving and sinful world. I also think, just as before the Flood, that God's patience has worn thin, and so are His people and even all of creation! *For we know that all creation has been groaning as in the pains of childbirth right up to the present time* (Romans 8:22 NLT).

God is love, but He's also holy. Those who have not accepted the substitute of Jesus' sacrifice on the cross will experience the horrors that nightmares are made of. An angry God and a desperate devil create scenarios that no imaginative science-fiction writer could even envision.

Persecution will reach a zenith during this time while the powers of darkness struggle in their fight against God's followers. *"Those who are wise will instruct many, though for a time they will fall by the sword or be burned or captured or plundered"* (Daniel 11:33 NLT). True believers are forced to go underground. If you are currently suffering persecution for being a Christ follower, hang in there. Joy comes in the morning and the victory is already won!

THE JUDGMENTS

After the Church is brought to heaven in the Rapture, Revelation explains the sequence of events with a series of seal, trumpet, and bowl judgments. The descriptions may be symbolic but their effect on the earth is oh-so literal. These judgments sound scary and they are, although if you are a child of God, everything is going to be okay.

They start as Jesus takes the scroll to read the judgments. *"You are worthy to take the scroll and break its seals and open it. For you were killed and your blood has ransomed people for God from every tribe and language and people and nation"* (Revelation 5:9 NLT).

The Four Horsemen of the Apocalypse arrive: (Revelation 6:2–8)

1st Seal	rider on a white horse	the Antichrist
2nd Seal	rider on a red horse	bloodshed from war
3rd Seal	rider on a black horse	famine
4th Seal	rider on a green horse	death of 1/4 population by war, famine, disease, wild animals

The Seals continue with spiritual and natural ramifications: (Revelation 6:9–17)

5th Seal	souls under the altar	martyrs
6th Seal	earthquakes, sky falls	fear grips the people
7th Seal	silence in heaven	starts trumpet judgments (144,000 Jews are sealed; martyrs cry out)

When the Lamb broke the seventh seal, there was silence throughout heaven for about half an hour. And I saw the seven angels who stand before God, and they were given seven trumpets (Revelation 8:1,2 NLT).

1st Trumpet	hail and fire, blood	1/3 of vegetation destroyed
2nd Trumpet	burning mountain in the sea	1/3 of sea becomes blood
3rd Trumpet	Wormwood falls from sky	1/3 of water is contaminated
4th Trumpet	heavenly bodies collide	1/3 of Earth's light is lost
5th Trumpet	locust-type demons	painful torture for five months
6th Trumpet	200 million army	1/3 of mankind is killed
7th Trumpet	little scroll, bowls	wrath of God increases

Then one of the four living creatures gave to the seven angels seven golden bowls full of the wrath of God who lives forever and ever (Revelation 15:7).

1st Bowl	horrible sores break out on anyone who has taken the mark of the beast
2nd Bowl	oceans turn to blood and everything in them dies
3rd Bowl	rivers and springs turn to blood
4th Bowl	heat from the sun scorches everything
5th Bowl	darkness covers the earth
6th Bowl	Euphrates River dries up so armies can march to Israel
7th Bowl	greatest earthquake and hailstorm with 75 lb. stones

These are the manifestations of God's great wrath on an unbelieving world. With God's help, you can survive this horrible time to repopulate the earth during the millennial Kingdom Age. *"And unless those days were shortened, no flesh would be saved; but for the elect's sake those days will be shortened"* (Matthew 24:22).

THE FOCUS ON ISRAEL

Israel is the "apple of God's eye" and a focal point during the Tribulation. In Jeremiah 30:7, the Tribulation is called the "time of Jacob's trouble." The history of the country can be summed up this way: Israel home; Israel scattered; Israel regathered; Israel isolated; Israel attacked; Israel saved.

As prophesied, Israel became a nation in a day (May 14, 1948), and millions of Jewish people have now returned to the homeland. It is a thriving country: irrigation has crops blooming, oil and natural gas have been discovered, and the nation is militarily and economically strong. But for the most part, and as I write this, the blinders are still on and the majority of God's chosen people do not accept Jesus as their Messiah. Events that happen during the Tribulation change all that. *"When those bitter days have come upon you far in the future, you will finally return to the Lord your God and listen to what He tells you. For the Lord your God is merciful—He will not abandon you or destroy you or forget the solemn*

SURVIVING THE TRIBULATION

covenant He made with your ancestors" (Deuteronomy 4:30-31 NLT).

• BATTLES. There are two, maybe three, major battles that involve Israel. Prior to the Gog and Magog War, it seems that Syria succeeds in causing harm to northern Israel; however, Israel strikes back and destroys Damascus. *Look. Damascus will disappear! It will become a heap of ruins. This is the just reward of those who plunder and destroy the people of God* (Isaiah 17:1,14 NLT).

The Gog and Magog War occurs sometime around the Rapture or beginning of the Tribulation. Explained in Ezekiel 38–39, Gog, a (demonic?) leader of Magog (Russia?), joins with its allies, among them Persia (Iran) and Libya to attack Israel for spoil (oil?). But God supernaturally turns the Russian federation against themselves and Israel succeeds, spiritually stronger knowing that God still works miracles on its behalf. *In the distant future, I will bring you Gog against my land as everyone watches, and my holiness will be displayed by what happens to you* (Ezekiel 38:16 NLT). The Bible says that the weapons will burn for seven years, the same time span as the Tribulation.

And of course, the ultimate Battle of Armageddon will occur at the end of the Tribulation. *And they gathered all the rulers and their armies to a place called Armageddon in Hebrew* (Revelation 16:16 NLT). On a large plain in Israel, also called the valley of Jezreel, the unholy trinity will gather all the nations together to defeat God. (Yes, God!) *I saw the beast, the kings of the earth, and their armies, gathered together to make war against Him who sat on the horse and against His army* (Revelation 19:19). That's when Jesus Christ returns and makes short work of that war.

Now I saw heaven opened, and behold, a white horse. And He who sat on him was called Faithful and True, and in righteousness He judges and makes war. His eyes were like a flame of fire, and on His head were many crowns. He had a name written that no one knew except Himself. He was clothed with a robe dipped in blood, and His name is called The Word of God. And the armies in heaven, clothed in fine linen, white and clean, followed Him on white horses. Now out of His mouth goes a sharp sword, that with it He should strike the nations. And He Himself will rule them with a rod of iron. He Himself treads the winepress of the fierceness and wrath of Almighty God. And He has on His robe and on His thigh a name written: KING OF KINGS AND LORD OF LORDS (Revelation 19:11–16).

• THE TEMPLE. The land of Israel is at the center of the world; Jerusalem is at the center of Israel; and the Temple is at the center of Jerusalem. It has been almost two thousand years since the Jewish people had a temple in Jerusalem to worship God and fulfill their traditional requirements. *Go and measure the Temple of God and the altar, and count the number of worshipers* (Revelation 11:1 NLT).

There is a deep longing in their souls to rebuild the third Temple. The Temple Institute has steadily been preparing the vestments, candelabra, bowls, and other vessels for readiness when the building is completed. (I wonder if the location of the Ark of the Covenant will be revealed.) The following statement appeared on the Temple Institute's fundraising website, "The Third Temple in Jerusalem will be the House of Prayer for all nations. Every prophet of Israel, without exception, prophesied that the Temple would be rebuilt, ushering in a new era of universal harmony and peace." Sounds like it fits right in with the New World Order way of thinking.

If you are living during the Tribulation period, the Temple is already standing. It needs to exist to serve as the location for the Antichrist to commit the abomination of desolation—sitting in the holiest part of the Temple and demanding worship, declaring himself to be god. *"So when you see the abomination of desolation spoken of by Daniel the prophet, standing where it ought not (let the reader understand) then let those who are in Judea flee to the mountains"* (Mark 13:14; also see Daniel 11:31).

A prior fulfillment of this occurred during the 175–164 BC reign of Antiochus IV Epiphanes when he set up an altar to Zeus and sacrificed pigs, thus defiling the Second Temple. He was a foreshadow of the Antichrist.

• ANTI-SEMITISM. Jerusalem is a "cup of trembling" to all the nations and anti-Semitism again rears its ugly head, which is an intense hatred for the Jewish people straight from Satan. Persecution is manifested first through radical Islam and finally by the global religion of the Antichrist. *And the dragon was enraged with the woman and he went to make war with the rest of her offspring, who keep the commandments of God and have the testimony of Jesus Christ* (Revelation 12:17).

After the abomination of desolation in the Temple, God has instructed the Jews to flee into the wilderness to escape the certain destruction of the Great Tribulation (Revelation 12:6; Matthew 24:15–20). This place in the wilderness may be the old stone fortress called Petra in the city of Bozrah in the land of Edom (currently Jordan) to the north (Micah 2:2).

• THE WITNESSES. Because the Church and the indwelling Holy Spirit leave Earth at the Rapture, God appoints two Jewish witnesses to preach the Gospel. *"And I will give power to my two witnesses, and they will be clothed in sackcloth and will prophesy during those 1,260 days* [3¹/₂ years] *"* (Revelation 11:3 NLT).

They have the power to kill with fire, shut up the skies to stop the rain, and call for any plague they like. When they complete their testimony, the Antichrist kills them and their bodies lie in the main street of Jerusalem for 3¹/₂ days, as all the world views their dead bodies (thanks to satellite and cable television!) giving presents to each other in celebration. But the Lord will resurrect them to heaven (see Revelation 11:3–12).

Could they possibly be Moses and Elijah? Moses represents the law and Elijah, the prophets. Moses turned water into blood, and it's interesting that Satan fought for his body (see Jude 1:9). Elijah was taken to heaven in a whirlwind without dying, plus he made it rain and called down fire during his ministry (see 2 Kings 1:10). They both appear with Christ at the Transfiguration. (Enoch, who went straight to heaven without dying before the Flood, is a type of raptured saint who never needs to die.)

Also during the Tribulation, after the sixth trumpet, God seals 144,000 Jews (12,000 from each of the twelve tribes) who accept Jesus as their Messiah, in order to keep them safe so they can spread the message of salvation. *Some of the Jews have hard hearts but this will last only until the complete number of Gentiles comes to Christ. And so all Israel will be saved* (Romans 11:25–26 NLT).

The 144,000 are described as being sealed, which could mean they are supernaturally protected from all evil. Unless God seals these witnesses for their protection, they will never live to preach more than one message—the seal makes them untouchable. This way they will be among those who survive the Tribulation to populate the millennial kingdom in their mortal bodies.

Since being sealed usually refers to the Holy Spirit, I believe that these witnesses will be the only ones in the Tribulation who are indwelt with the Spirit. During this time, post-rapture salvation for the Jews looks more like Old Testament salvation, but instead of looking forward to the Cross, the Tribulation believers will look back to the Cross. People have always been saved by faith, but this isn't the Age of Grace anymore. There has to be evidence of that faith by obedience to the law. *Here is the patience of the saints; here are those who keep the commandments of God and the faith of Jesus* (Revelation 14:12).

THE NEW WORLD ORDER

When it comes to government maintaining order out of chaos, society usually chooses one of two idioms. Either it strives for liberty and freedom, trusting the individual to do the right thing, or it seeks to take control for the greater good of the masses. That's how dictatorships develop—taking advantage of a society when it's going through a rough patch. Well, the Tribulation is more than just a rough patch, and there is a dictator who is out to control every human being on the planet. I'm talking g-l-o-b-a-l—once again, a New World Order (NWO). In 1939, H.G. Wells said, "Countless people will hate the New World Order and will die protesting against it." In 1939!!

Its goal is to create a one-world government, a one-world economy, a one-world religion, and a one-world police force—all in the name of peace, safety, and security. Population control. Total control. Its agenda is already detailed in documents from the United Nations, Trilateral Commission, Bilderberg Group, World Bank, and Council of Foreign Relations. (I've already mentioned some of their activities in Chapter 3 under "Globalization.") On October 24, 2011, the Associated Press reported, "A proposal by the Vatican's Pontifical Council for Justice and Peace calls for a new world economic order based on ethics and the achievement of a universal common good."

The earliest attempt at global government, which followed the Great Flood, was Nimrod and his Tower of Babel (Genesis 11). To humble man's pride and with knowledge that unity would change the order of things before its time, God separated the one-world builders by giving them different languages, thus driving them to diverse places around the globe. There they fiercely defended their nations from nearby invaders. For most of history, civilizations on the other side of the world were strange and exotic, and, except for travelling storytellers, not much was known about far-flung places. The inventions of air travel and communications technology have progressed to where no part of the world is inaccessible, creating a global community.

Before long, society questioned everything, especially authority, religion, and even history. Revisionists have rewritten history books to suit their agenda. Science became subjective ("junk science"), utilizing observation in lieu of hard facts to justify more regulations. For instance, global warming became a political issue instead of just a theory, moving governments to enact legislation banning certain businesses from operating, adding prohibitive regulations and excessive taxation, driving them right out of existence.

Control is already here when we need a certificate to be born and to die, a license to fish, a registration to drive, a permit to build, a number to get a job, a fingerprint to cash a check, and a passport to travel.

When the economies of the world tanked in 2008, governments bought up private enterprises and instituted sweeping regulations, and markets moved to a more global system. What happens on the New York Stock Exchange affects the markets in Japan. Oil prices in the Middle East affect many of us. A one-currency, world system is next.

Ecumenism attempts to unite religions, to be accepting of everyone's beliefs because it is an accepted mindset that peace is the ultimate objective and tolerance is the highest virtue. World leaders stress that only a "new world order" can save us.

There have been four major world empires: Babylonian, Medo-Persian, Grecian, and Roman. According to the Bible, the Antichrist arises from some form of a revived Roman Empire to lead the world into a temporary peace, first as the leader of a ten-nation confederacy and then as the final New World Order: Babylon—the Empire of Antichrist.

The first President of the U.N. General Assembly (1946–1947) and Secretary General of NATO (1957–1961), Paul-Henri Spaak, famously said, "We do not want another committee, we have too many already. What we want is a man of sufficient stature to hold the allegiance of all people, and to lift us out of the economic morass into which we are sinking. Send us such a man, and be he god or devil, we will receive him."[1]

In the wake of the Rapture and other last-days chaos, the world is primed to accept the New World Order. Mankind has spent centuries since the Tower of Babel circumventing God's intervention. The one-world drive is once again the supreme goal, which ultimately comes to fruition under the final (earthly) global leader, the Antichrist.

THE UNHOLY TRINITY:
Satan, Antichrist, and False Prophet

And I saw three unclean spirits like frogs coming out of the mouth of the dragon, out of the mouth of the beast and out of the mouth of the false prophet (Revelation 16:13).

Since his fall, Satan's goal is to be worshiped as a god. He is jealous of Jesus and pride brings out the very worst in him. As the father of lies, his greatest trick and weapon is deception—to get people to believe he doesn't exist, or even that he can be "fun." Society fails to mention the devil except as entertainment in horror movies or at Halloween—and then he's basically a cartoon character. Not someone to take seriously. In fact, films depicting evil and sadistic violence are tops at the box office, and Satan is laughing all the way to the bank.

Next the Devil took him (Jesus) to the peak of a very high mountain and showed him the nations of the world and all their glory. "I will give it all to you," he said, "if you will only kneel down and worship me." "Get out of here

Satan," Jesus told him. "For the Scriptures say, 'You must worship the Lord your God and serve only Him'" (Matthew 4:8–10 NLT). Satan claimed that he had authority over the earth's kingdoms and Jesus didn't correct him, but instead used the Sword of Truth (the Word of God) to defeat him. But if Satan can give the kingdoms of the world to whomever he wishes, it only reasons that weak men will sell their souls for such power. Ungodly leaders and evil rulers have sadly become the norm instead of the exception.

During the Tribulation, Satan is barred from heaven and is thrown to the earth to cause his final and most intense mischief. *Then there was war in heaven. Michael and the angels fought the dragon and his angels. And the dragon lost the battle and was forced out of heaven. This great dragon—the ancient serpent called the Devil or Satan, the one deceiving the whole world—was thrown down to the earth with all his angels* (Revelation 12:7–9 NLT). Then a voice shouts in heaven that terror comes on the earth and sea because Satan comes down with great anger, and he knows that his time is now short. He may actually possess the Antichrist.

Even those who have never cracked open a Bible have heard about the Antichrist and his number, 666. *Let the one who has understanding solve the number of the beast, for it is the number of a man. His number is 666* (Revelation 13:18). The word Antichrist has a double meaning: "against Christ" and "instead of Christ"—the ultimate counterfeit messiah. Just as Satan is sometimes referred to as the dragon, the Antichrist is referred to as the beast. The spirit of Antichrist is rebellion and the motivation behind anti-Semitism and anti-Christianity.

So, with chaos running rampant on the earth after the Rapture, this man arises on the world stage (most likely out of a Revived Roman Empire) who is a smooth talker, cunning, and able to make peace between Israel and her enemies. His number is 666, which is the riddle of the ages. His charisma makes him very popular and even loved, magic tricks make him seem powerful, and the people of the world look to him as a savior. *And all the people who belonged to this world worshiped the beast* (Revelation 13:8 NLT). He may even identify himself as Jesus Christ. Without the grace of God, the majority of people are deceived into believing a great lie. He may claim to be an alien, a higher being. Those living during the Tribulation know his identity.

This evil man will come to do the work of Satan with counterfeit power and signs and miracles. He will use every kind of wicked deception to fool those who are on their way to destruction because they refuse to believe the truth that would save them (2 Thessalonians 2:9,10 NLT).

Some of the traits of the Antichrist:

- Intellectual and boastful (Daniel 7:20)
- No regard for the god of women or any god of his ancestors (Daniel 11:37)
- He will honor a god of fortresses (Daniel 11:38)
- Assyrian (part of the eastern Roman Empire) (Isaiah 10:12–15)
- European (part of the western Roman Empire) (Daniel 9:26,27)
- Man of lawlessness and son of perdition (2 Thessalonians 2:3)
- One who comes in his own name (John 5:43)
- Beast from the sea (of humanity?) (Revelation 13)
- The little horn (Daniel 7:8–11)
- One who works signs and wonders (2 Thessalonians 2:9)

The nature and goal of the Antichrist changes as he drops the charade in the middle of the Tribulation. He breaks the peace treaty with Israel and the Jews are again subject to intense persecution. The Antichrist is "assassinated" but appears to be raised back to life by Satan in an attempt to counterfeit the resurrection of Jesus Christ. *And I saw one of his heads as if it had been mortally wounded, and his deadly wound was healed. And all the world marveled and followed the beast* (Revelation 13:3). Under his dictatorship, the world moves toward a single government with one economy and one religion.

The False Prophet is a religious leader who administers the global religion based on worship of the Antichrist, and is his "right-hand man." The False Prophet uses sorcery and/or technology (hologram?) to create an image of the beast that can speak and he demands that all who will not worship the image be killed. *He was permitted to give life to the statue so that it could speak. Then the statue commanded that anyone refusing to worship it must die* (Revelation 13:15 NLT). The Antichrist actually stands in the holy place of the Jewish Temple and declares himself god. This abomination of desolation marks a turning point in the Tribulation.

The False Prophet institutes the "mark of the beast," a form of identification placed on/in the forehead or the right hand, signifying allegiance to the Antichrist. *He required everyone—great and small, rich and poor, slave and free—to be given a mark on the right hand or on the forehead. And no one could buy or sell anything without that mark, which was either the name of the beast or the number of his name* (Revelation 13:16 NLT). It's interesting to note that in the King James Version of the Bible, the verse is "in the right hand or in the forehead"— a clearer expression of a biochip inserted under the skin, or a tattoo which instills ink into the skin. The location of this mark is significant when you consider that God told the Israelites to bind His laws to their hands and wear them on their foreheads (Deuteronomy 6:8).

In a cashless society with an economy that is under the total control of a dictator, it is impossible to buy or sell anything without the mark. This means that anyone who doesn't worship the Antichrist is cut off from the global economy, making it almost impossible to earn a living and obtain basic necessities—food for your children or medicine for your sick mother. With such technology, the Antichrist controls the world's commerce with total sway over the population. His great computers know where everyone is at all times, as the mark contains a global positioning system and his eyes in the sky (satellites) and patrolling x-ray trucks (think Google Earth on steroids) and drones or through your smart phone cameras (or some supernatural system) watch every move. The proverbial "Big Brother." The technology is now available to accomplish this!

The Antichrist actually helps in the division of the "sheep and goats" as anyone who worships the beast and accepts the mark chooses death for eternity. Those who reject the mark will die, most likely by decapitation (Revelation 20:4) or will be forced to scavenge and barter to survive. There is no indication of any opportunity for repentance after accepting the mark of the beast, and as a result is a very significant turning point in a person's life during the Tribulation. Do not take the mark!

BABYLON THE GREAT

Babylon the Great is the wealthy, immoral, corrupt, apostate, post-modern civilization of the Tribulation. As I write this, it's not clear if Babylon refers to an apostate Christian religion, a Muslim caliphate, Catholic or New Age goddess worship, a code word for a revived Roman Empire, the New World Order, or a metaphor for a worldwide system of evil. Like "Wall Street" describes the whole American financial system, it may be the same with Mystery Babylon.

It is possible that the literal ancient city of Babylon is rebuilt because the Antichrist is supposedly from Assyria (modern-day Iraq) and Babylon is mentioned 280 times in the Bible—present at the very beginning of history. It's interesting that God divided mankind with different languages at the Tower of Babel (Babylon); so it is fitting that it would come full circle, back to the original land of unity.

Nimrod was the first world ruler, reigning from Babylon in Shinar (Mesopotamia). By 600 BC, King Nebuchadnezzar had built Babylon into a pagan empire, a center of religion, government, and commerce. Isaiah and Jeremiah predicted its end and Babylon fell in one night to the armies of Cyrus the Persian in 539 BC and has remained in ruins. Saddam Hussein attempted to rebuild it until he was overthrown in 2003, and interest persists in recapturing the former glory of Babylon.

And on her forehead a name was written: MYSTERY, BABYLON THE GREAT, THE MOTHER OF HARLOTS AND OF THE ABOMINATIONS OF THE EARTH. I saw the woman, drunk with the blood of the saints and with the blood of the martyrs of Jesus. And when I saw her, I marveled with great amazement (Revelation 17:5).

Babylon is fallen—that great city is fallen! She has become the hideout of demons and evil spirits, a nest for filthy buzzards and a den for dreadful beasts. For all the nations have drunk the wine of her immorality (Revelation 18:2-3 NLT).

Since it is called Mystery Babylon, I believe it's not the ancient city in Iraq that is referred to. Babylon, whether literal or figurative, falls forever at Armageddon. *"For the Lord is destroying Babylon. He will silence her"* (Jeremiah 51:55 NLT).

What about America? Some have suggested that the United States is Mystery Babylon with its multitudes, greed, and big cities with major seaports. It's possible although improbable. The United States is not mentioned in Revelation, which is surprising since it has been such a super power, was instrumental in the creation of the nation of Israel, and has been the main disseminator of the Gospel message through missionaries and satellite television. A shining city on a hill and incredibly blessed by God with abundant resources, peace, prosperity, and unity. However, the America I grew up in is not the America I live in now—it is on a downward spiral due to poor management, ignorance, blatant sin, and that aforementioned greed.

I like to think that America falls into oblivion because the Rapture removes enough of the population that chaos ensues; or maybe the economy collapses and we become a third-world country; or maybe nuclear war or natural disasters wipe us out. Or just maybe, we are Mystery Babylon.

Most likely it's our sins as a nation that reduce us to nothing more than a cog in the wheel of the one-world government.

THE BATTLE OF ARMAGEDDON

As history races toward its conclusion, the end of the Tribulation is in sight at the Battle of Armageddon—the mother of all battles and the last world war. The Antichrist and his allies assemble with the intent of finally destroying the remainder of God's people and His city, Jerusalem. The Bible teaches that this war will involve not only the whole land of Israel but also all the nations of the world.

"And it shall happen in that day that I will make Jerusalem a very heavy stone for all peoples; all who would heave it away will surely be cut in pieces, though all nations of the earth are gathered against it" (Zechariah 12:3).

The nations' armies gather in northern Israel around the hill of Megiddo, in the Valley of Jezreel, also called Jehosephat (which happens to mean 'the Lord judges'). This vast open space between Haifa and Jerusalem is the perfect setting, with the kings of the east (China?) able to cross over the now dried-up Euphrates River to join the armies of the Antichrist.

Why do the nations rage? Why do the people waste their time with futile plans? The kings of the earth prepare for battle; the rulers plot together against the Lord and His anointed one. Let us break their chains, they cry, and free ourselves from this slavery. But the One who rules in heaven laughs. The Lord scoffs at them. Then in anger He rebukes them, terrifying them with his fierce fury (Psalm 2:1–5 NLT).

As the Antichrist leads the battle against Jerusalem, great natural disturbances occur, the earth quakes, and the sun is darkened. The campaign includes Christ destroying Babylon (Revelation 18), leading out the Jews who are in Bozrah (Micah 2:2), and winning the battle itself. The outcome of this great battle is already known and has been known for thousands of years. *And I saw the beast, the kings of the earth, and their armies, gathered together to make war against Him who sat on the horse and against His army* (Revelation 19:19).

The true Messiah, Jesus Christ, returns to Earth riding on a white horse and leading the armies of heaven—the angels and saints dressed in white and riding on white horses. As we know, Jesus is victorious. *The armies of heaven, dressed in pure white linen, followed him on white horses. From his mouth came a sharp sword and with it he struck down the nations…and trod the winepress of the fierce wrath of almighty God* (Revelation 19:14–15 NLT). *Both the beast and his false prophet were thrown alive into the lake of fire that burns with sulfur. Their entire army was killed by the sharp sword that came out of the mouth of the one riding the white horse. And all the vultures of the sky gorged themselves on the dead bodies* (Revelation 19:20–21 NLT).

Now Enoch, who lived seven generations after Adam, prophesied, "Look, the Lord is coming with thousands of his holy ones. He will bring the people of the world to judgment. He will convict the ungodly of all the evil things they have done in rebellion and of all the insults that godless sinners have spoken against him" (Jude 1:14,15 NLT).

This battle will be the bloodiest event in human history as the forces of good and evil come to the ultimate confrontation. *And the wine press was trodden outside the city, and blood came out from the wine press up to the horses' bridles for a distance of two hundred miles* (Revelation 14:20 NLT).

THE SECOND COMING

The Second Coming of Christ (Act II) to the earth is an event long antici-
pated. It is the culmination of the annals of history. The moment when
every eye shall see, every knee shall bow, and every tongue confess that Jesus
Christ is Lord. Hallelujah!

*"Then the sign of the Son of Man will appear in heaven, and then all the
tribes of the earth will mourn, and they will see the Son of Man coming on the
clouds of heaven with power and great glory"* (Matthew 24:30). *Behold, He is
coming with clouds, and every eye will see Him, even they who pierced Him.
And all the tribes of the earth will mourn because of Him. Even so, Amen* (Revelation 1:7).

As Jesus' foot touches down on the Mount of Olives, the earth is split,
and Jesus takes His rightful place as King of kings and Lord of lords.

The Second Coming of Christ is necessary to:

- Reveal Himself and His own (saints and angels)
- Save Israel and the remnant of believers
- Defeat God's enemies
- Judge the beast and false prophet; send them to the lake of fire
- Bind Satan for a thousand years
- Judge the nations
- Redeem creation
- Establish His Millennial Kingdom

After the Battle of Armageddon at His return, Jesus restores the nation
of Israel, separates the "sheep from the goats," resurrects the Tribulation and
Old Testament saints, cleanses the earth, hands out assignments, constructs
the millennial Temple, and ushers in the mortal survivors. There may be a
gap of time (45 days?) between Armageddon and the Millennium for all of
this to occur (Daniel 12:11–12).

The Marriage Supper of the Lamb takes place either in heaven during
the Tribulation, or, I think, at the beginning of the Millennium so that the
Tribulation and Old Testament saints can be included. What a celebration

that will be! *Let us be glad and rejoice and honor him. For the time has come for the wedding feast of the Lamb and his bride has prepared herself. And the angel said, "Write this: Blessed are those who are invited to the wedding feast of the Lamb"* (Revelation 19:7–9 NLT).

Yes, the Second Coming of Christ will ultimately bring about a thousand-year Kingdom, a time of peace and a glorious respite from years and years of strife and strivings, where the lion will lie down with the lamb. I can hardly wait!

And every creature which is in heaven and on the earth and under the earth and such as are in the sea, and all that are in them, I heard saying: "Blessing and honor and glory and power be to Him who sits on the throne, and to the Lamb, forever and ever!" (Revelation 5:13).

Chapter 6
FROM THE KINGDOM TO ETERNITY

With God in charge, I believe everything will work out for the best in the end.

HENRY FORD

The Second Coming of Christ to the Mount of Olives essentially ends the Tribulation and the world as we've known it. Those who have been martyred during the Tribulation by taking a stand for Jesus will join their already-resurrected brothers and sisters from the Church Age with their own resurrected bodies to reign with Christ. The Old Testament saints will also be resurrected—I believe they are the guests at the Marriage Feast, along with the believing mortals who have endured and physically survived the Tribulation. God will sort the survivors: the believers to populate the Kingdom and the unbelievers to Hades with the rest of the unbelieving dead, to await their Final Judgment at the Great White Throne after the thousand-year Kingdom Age. Satan will be bound in the bottomless pit for the thousand years, allowing an idyllic and peaceful time on the earth.

THE MILLENNIUM KINGDOM

The central focus of the Millennium is Jesus Christ who will physically rule from Jerusalem. It is His time of manifestation, His time of glory, of revelation, of bringing the earth back to its original purpose. Justice will prevail, nature will behave, and longevity of life for the mortals will be the norm. The Bible states that this will be a time of perfect peace.

For unto us a Child is born, unto us a Son is given; and the government will be upon His shoulder. And His name will be called Wonderful, Counselor, Mighty God, Everlasting Father, Prince of Peace. Of the increase of His government and peace there will be no end. Upon the throne of David and over His kingdom, to order it and establish it with judgment and justice from that time forward, ever forever. The zeal of the Lord of hosts will perform this (Isaiah 9:6–7).

The already-resurrected saints will reign with Christ, redeemed to their full potential, assisting Him in the daily concerns of running a kingdom. Work will bring prosperity and fulfillment, and people will live out each day with real joy. Learning will expand as God reveals His knowledge to us and the redeemed earth will bring beauty beyond our imaginations. There will be so much to know, people to see and visit, universes to rule, true enjoyment of God and Earth. *Everyone will live quietly in their own homes in peace and prosperity for there will be nothing to fear. The LORD Almighty has promised this!* (Micah 4:4).

From the severe earthquakes at the end of the Tribulation, the earth's landscape will change, as every mountain will be lowered, every valley lifted and island moved. Jerusalem and Mount Zion will be set on a high hill, able to be seen from a distance. The vapor canopy may be restored allowing for the longer life spans and lush vegetation.

Animals will be tame, and the lion will lie down with the lamb. *"The wolf also shall dwell with the lamb, the leopard shall lie down with the young goat, the calf and the young lion and the fatling together;...and the lion shall eat straw like the ox, the nursing child shall play by the cobra's hole, and the weaned child shall put his hand in the viper's den. They shall not hurt nor destroy in all My holy mountain, for the earth shall be full of the knowledge of the LORD as the waters cover the sea"* (Isaiah 11:6–9).

Whenever I get to feeling down, my mind imagines how wonderful this time will be. I dream about reuniting with my believing loved ones. That I can sing in tune and reach the high notes for worship or canter on the back of a majestic horse through fields of gold. No more fear of heights. No more fear at all! No more pain, sin, crying, sickness, loneliness, war, or despair. Lord, give me patience because I seriously long for those days of bliss. *But those who wait on the LORD shall renew their strength; they shall mount up with wings like eagles, they shall run and not be weary, they shall walk and not faint* (Isaiah 40:31).

The Millennium is God's time for keeping His Word, rewarding His people, demonstrating His righteousness, fulfilling the covenants, and adding more people to eternity. Those who populate the kingdom will have natural, mortal bodies, and so will eat and procreate, producing children and living long lives. It also seems to be a buffer age between this unholy earth and a holy eternity.

The devil is let loose again after the thousand years are up. At that time, it will be revealed just how unregenerate humankind's hearts are, as many again believe the lies of Satan and follow him in his final revolt against God. But this time, fire comes down from heaven and consumes the armies of Satan. No need for a messy battle this time around. *The devil, who deceived them, was cast into the lake of fire and brimstone where the beast and the false prophet are. And they will be tormented day and night forever and ever* (Revelation 20:10).

After the Millennium, all people are resurrected—some to eternal life and the others to eternal death. It's Judgment Day at the Great White Throne where Jesus Christ will judge every man or woman who didn't accept His offer of salvation. Because the blood of Jesus did not cover their sins, their names are not in the Book of Life. *And anyone not found written in the Book of Life was cast into the lake of fire* (Revelation 20:15).

A FEW WORDS ABOUT HELL

Many people do not believe that hell is a reality. It's uncomfortable to even think about, so they'd rather just ignore it and hope it goes away. But that won't happen. Hell is a vital motivation for people to run toward grace and a just means of punishment for those who refuse God. They wonder why a loving God could send His creatures to such a nasty place, but it's not God who sends anyone there. By rejecting the free gift of heaven through Jesus, each person makes his or her own choice to go to hell.

If everyone has a free pass to heaven, then why did Jesus have to die? If everyone went to heaven, there would be no proof of faith. If everyone went to heaven, there would be no incentive for choosing the straight and narrow path. *"The highway to hell is broad and its gate is wide for the many who choose the easy way. But the gateway to life is small and the road is narrow, and only a few ever find it"* (Matthew 7:13–14 NLT).

And if everyone went to heaven, then God would fail to be just, and justice needs to be meted out. Our sense of fairness demands it. Christ will say to those who are not covered by His blood, *"Depart from Me, you cursed, into the everlasting fire prepared for the devil and his angels"* (Matthew 25:41).

We have been given glimpses of hell straight from the pages of Scripture, as well as from witnesses who have either come back from near-death experiences or were privy to special revelation. It isn't pretty. Doctors who have revived patients recount the total panic of a person who has seen just a bit of hell and many turn their lives to Christ afterward.

In *23 Minutes in Hell*, Bill Wiese claims God allowed him to spend twenty-three minutes in hell. He describes his experience as a warning for everyone; the descriptions are quite horrifying and consistent with biblical pictures. Here's some of what you'll find in hell:

- Separation from God and loved ones
- Constant thirst
- Hardly any air; foul smell
- Physical, emotional, and mental weakness
- Nakedness
- Hopelessness
- Darkness, except for the glow of fires in the distance
- Inability to sleep or rest, or die
- Chained in prison or dungeons
- Maggots eating flesh that's never consumed
- Bullied and tortured by monstrous demons
- Unbearable heat
- Endless screaming, weeping, and gnashing of teeth

"Father Abraham, have some pity! Send Lazarus to dip the tip of his finger in water and cool my tongue because I am in anguish in these flames" (Luke 16:24 NLT).

Hell is a real place, most likely located in the lower parts of the earth. *He descended into the lower parts of the earth* (Ephesians 4:9) and *hell from beneath* (Isaiah 14:9). There are stories about the gates of hell, openings in the earth, temporary passageways. There is also evidence that there are different levels of hell, a la Dante's *Inferno*, who imagined a sign above the gate of hell reading, "Abandon hope, all ye who enter here."

Sheol is a term meaning *grave*, and Hades is the place where unbelievers' souls go until their resurrection. There is no purgatory, unless you call it Earth. The pit or bottomless pit is where Satan and friends are chained for the thousand years. Hell, Gehenna (a garbage dump, inferring that those who reject God are like trash) or the lake of fire is the final destination for all unbelieving humans and rebellious angels. *And death and the grave were thrown into the lake of fire. This is the second death – the lake of fire. And anyone whose name was not found recorded in the Book of Life was thrown into the lake of fire* (Revelation 20:14–15 NLT).

Satan and his demons hate the creation of God and seek to destroy it. *Be sober, be vigilant, because your adversary the devil walks about like a roaring lion, seeking whom he may devour* (1 Peter 5:8). These enemies of God and mankind are known by the wars they start, the hatred they promote, the evil they whisper in the ear, the murders they initiate, the lies they tell, the opposition to God and His ways. They are dedicated to destruction and have obvious motives for promoting hell's nonexistence. If we don't believe it exists, we won't bother doing what it takes to avoid it. And we won't warn our friends either.

Hell is not a place you ever want to be. Just because we find it all so weird doesn't mean it doesn't exist. God's ways are not our ways. *"I'll tell you whom to fear. Fear God, who has the power to kill people and then throw them into hell"* (Luke 12:5 NLT).

A free ticket to hell, without passing Go, is to accept the mark of the beast. *If anyone worships the beast and his image, and receives his mark on his forehead or on his hand, he himself shall also drink of the wine of the wrath of God, which is poured out full strength into the cup of His indignation. He shall be tormented with fire and brimstone in the presence of the holy angels and in the presence of the Lamb. And the smoke of their torment ascends forever and ever, and they have no rest day or night, who worship the beast and his image, and whoever receives the mark of his name* (Revelation 14:9–11).

But the heavens and the earth which are now preserved by the same word, are reserved for fire until the day of judgment and perdition of ungodly men (2 Peter 3:7).

Ignoring the subject won't make it go away. The only thing that will make hell go away is repenting and accepting God's offer of salvation through Jesus Christ. It is our responsibility to trust Him enough to exercise faith and obedience, to have a holy fear of God and to accept His free gift of heaven.

FINALLY, THE NEW HEAVEN AND THE NEW EARTH

Then, hallelujah!

After the Kingdom Age, God reveals the New Heaven and the New Earth. The former things will have passed away. *"For behold, I create new heavens and a new earth; and the former shall not be remembered or come to mind"* (Isaiah 65:17). Every civilization has expressed the need and longing for a heaven, Utopia, Shangri-la, paradise—a happily-ever-after. We have an ache inside us for a better place. Similar to the Garden of Eden, the New Earth will be the perfect environment for us: an actual place with abundant love, fulfillment, and beauty. Even now, when we catch a brief glimpse of beauty, whether a sunset, baby, flower, kitten, man, woman, or a particular landscape, we feel a sense of awe and can hardly contain a smile. We just feel that it's right. It will be more than we can even imagine. *Eye has not seen, nor ear heard, nor have entered into the heart of man the things which God has prepared for those who love Him* (1 Corinthians 2:9). We've only experienced nature under the curse and our imaginations run wild at what animals and plants could be like when redeemed. I think the animals will talk and sunflowers will grow to enormous size! We will shine forevermore in the presence and service of God!

And I saw a new heaven and a new earth, for the first heaven and the first earth had passed away. Also there was no more sea (Revelation 21:1).

The Bible teaches that there will no longer be any seas between the continents because all we'll need is the River of Living Water flowing from Jerusalem to tributaries everywhere. The Holy City of Jerusalem will be filled with the glory of God, with gates of pearl, streets of gold, walls of sparkling gems. The Tree of Life is also there. The size of the city is described as being an approximate 1,400-mile cube or pyramid. And there will be no darkness. *The city does not need the sun or the moon to shine on it, for the glory of God gives it light, and the Lamb is its lamp* (Revelation 21:23).

And most glorious of all, God the Father will be right there. *Look, the home of God is now among His people! God himself will be with them. He will remove all of their sorrows, and there will be no more death or sorrow or crying or pain. For the old world and its evils are gone forever* (Revelation 21:3–4). After all, it is this hope for eternal life that has burned in humankind's hearts since the day we were created. Our souls yearn for our Creator, and our hearts long for a place like our eternal home. The thought of just getting a hug from God keeps me going. The rest is all gravy.

When times get rough—and they will—keep your eyes on the prize. You can be comforted with thoughts of the New Heaven and New Earth—the reward for your faith, patience, and steadfastness. *"But he who endures to the end shall be saved"* (Matthew 24:13).

Part Two
SURVIVAL STRATEGIES

Chapter 7

TO DIE OR NOT TO DIE? THAT IS THE QUESTION!

*We cannot truly face life until we face the fact that
it will be taken away from us.*

BILLY GRAHAM

This book is entitled *Surviving the Tribulation,* so why is there a whole chapter on the question of dying? Although it is possible to make it out of the Tribulation physically alive, the sad fact is the majority of people will die.

It sounds like an oxymoron, but one of the main tenets of Christianity is that if we cling to our earthly lives too tightly, we will lose our eternal life. *"Whoever seeks to save his life will lose it, and whoever loses his life will preserve it"* (Luke 17:33). If you believe that God is real and that He is orchestrating the events of the Tribulation, then you need not fear death. In fact, if people fear death so much that they would do anything to avoid it, even to the point of worshiping a false idol, it means they don't understand what happened at the Cross or believe the resurrection. They will forfeit their very souls.

Death is a word that people don't want to talk about, or even think about. We talk about passing away, kicking the bucket, pushing up daisies, biting the dust, buying the farm, or croaking. Changing the language doesn't make death better, and ignoring it won't make it go away. Except for the dear saints who are alive at the Rapture, everyone will die at some point.

Unfortunately for the human race, there is much death during the Tribulation and many methods in which to die. I'm sure you've heard about someone who met his or her end in a weird or unexpected way. Accidents happen. Then there's the natural disasters, society's violence, pestilence and illness, suicide, starvation, wars. Now add weird science, the wrath of God, chaos vs. total control, and demonic attacks.

Then I heard a loud voice shouting across the heavens, "It has happened at last – the salvation and power and kingdom of our God, and the authority of his Christ! For the Accuser has been thrown down to earth—the one who accused our brothers and sisters before our God day and night. And they have defeated him because of the blood of the Lamb and because of their testimony. And they were not afraid to die. Rejoice, O heavens! And you who live in the heavens, rejoice! But terror will come on the earth and the sea. For the Devil has come down to you in great anger, and he knows that he has little time" (Revelation 12:10–12 NLT).

When the Holy Spirit leaves the earth at the Rapture, and especially after Satan is thrown out of heaven around the middle of the Tribulation, all hell literally breaks loose. Evil knows no bounds and manifests itself in various ways, and one of his major *modus operandi* is persecution of God's people.

Stay alert! Watch out for your great enemy, the devil. He prowls around like a roaring lion, looking for someone to devour (1 Peter 5:8 NLT).

Demonic deception is at an all-time high. You may already be brainwashed with propaganda regularly spewing from television sets, the Internet, and in the schools. A desensitization to evil is occurring, Like a frog that doesn't think to jump out of the pot when it's slowly heating until it boils to death, subtle changes over the past few decades have caused major shifts in attitudes resulting in death—death of people and death of ideologies.

Christianity—the greatest story ever told—is often a laughingstock of late-night comedy shows. Christians are the only group of people that it's permissible to be intolerant of— except for the Jews who've always had a hard time of it. The enemies of truth rewrite history and replace the facts with falsehoods, such as saying that the Holocaust never happened. This is a lie to blind the masses so they can't learn from past mistakes, thus allowing another dictator who promises peace, justice, and prosperity to terrorize us with brutality, war, and enslavement. Hitler was nothing compared to the power and devilry of the Antichrist.

The coming of the lawless one is according to the working of Satan, with all power, signs and lying wonders, and with all unrighteous deception among those who perish, because they did not receive the love of the truth, that they might be saved (2 Thessalonians 2:9).

Deception is an old tool of evil, and there's a fool born every minute. An illusionist's First Rule is "people are stupid." The devil is not. He'll use fear to immobilize you, temptations to make you sin, disease to weaken you, and untruths to bend your faith. It is very important to test every report with Scripture. I do believe that God can protect the integrity of His Word; however, an old worn out Bible is probably the most reliable! Visit regularly with other believers but beware of apostasy, that is, beliefs that have turned the truth of God's Word into a different message.

Let God's curse fall on anyone, including myself, who preaches any other message than the Good News of Christ. Even if an angel comes from heaven and preaches any other message, let him be forever cursed (Galatians 1:8 NLT).

Those who come to faith in Christ during the seven-year period are called Tribulation saints, and a huge number will be saved. Revelation 7:9 describes the number as a *"great multitude which no man could number."* These saints face a strong likelihood of being martyred under the Antichrist's demonic rule. *And he had power to give life unto the image of the beast, that the image of the beast should both speak and cause that as many as would not worship the image of the beast should be killed* (Revelation 13:15 NLT).

If you refuse to accept the mark of the beast and worship his image, the authorities will execute you, most likely by beheading. You may have family and friends who take the mark and, in their devotion to the Antichrist or his ideology, reject you and report you to the authorities. *"Brother will betray brother to death, fathers will betray their own children, and children will rise against their parents and cause them to be killed. And everyone will hate you because of your allegiance to me. But those who endure to the end will be saved"* (Mark 13:12).

If you accept the mark or bow down to worship the image, you will have made your choice to reject God and you will face His judgment—eternal death. The taking of the mark is a spiritual conversion from which there is no going back.

WHAT NOT TO BELIEVE

Now, you have been warned. Under any circumstances:

• DO NOT BELIEVE that the Antichrist is the Messiah. He may seem to rise from the dead, create peace on the earth, and perform amazing tricks, but he is not Jesus Christ. He is an imposter. The next time Earth-dwellers physically see Jesus, He will be returning in the clouds of heaven with His saints and angels at the Battle of Armageddon, and everyone will confess that Jesus Christ is the Lord. *Behold, He is coming with clouds and every eye will see Him, even they who pierced Him* (Revelation 1:7).

So if someone tells you, "Look, the Messiah is out in the desert," don't bother to go and look. Or, "Look he is hiding here," don't believe it! For as the lightning lights up the entire sky, so it will be when the Son of Man comes (Matthew 24:26–27 NLT).

• DO NOT BELIEVE any other message of salvation except for the Gospel, which briefly states: God became man in the perfect person of Jesus Christ, who loved us so much that He willingly suffered and died as a sacrifice in our place for our sins and was resurrected to life. He offers us the free gift of salvation if we will accept it. *"For God so loved the world that He gave His only begotten Son, that whoever believes in Him should not perish but have everlasting life"* (John 3:16).

• DO NOT BELIEVE history books, the media, the government, or any other source that denies the previous bullet's message. You can't even believe what you see. During the Tribulation deception is the key word. Be discerning!

CONQUERING FEAR

If you are living your life from an earthly perspective, you will be in fear—fear of losing your belongings, your loved ones, your health, your financial assets, your self-esteem, your freedom, and your life. It's only natural to be concerned with what's going on here. But if you're going to fear something or someone, then fear God—not so much being afraid of Him as taking Him seriously, respecting His authority, and knowing that only He has the power over your eternal life. *"And do not fear those who kill the body but cannot kill the soul. But rather fear Him who is able to destroy both soul and body in hell"* (Matthew 10:28).

Living with a heavenly perspective allows you to bear the sufferings of the Tribulation, knowing that it can't last for more than seven years, and then comes amazing joy! *"In fact, unless that time of calamity is shortened, the entire human race will be destroyed. But it will be shortened for the sake of God's chosen ones"* (Matthew 24:22 NLT).

There's an interesting verse that I've often used to comfort those who have lost loved ones, which opens a window into God's thoughts that we don't always see. *The righteous pass away, the godly often die before their time, and no one seems to care or wonder why. No one seems to understand that God is protecting them from the evil to come* (Isaiah 57:1). Although there is evil now, it will get worse, and you never know if God is actually using a death to spare that person even more grief and misery. If they have been saved by faith in Jesus, of course.

There have been Christian martyrs throughout Church history, starting with the apostles. If Jesus' closest friends died for the faith, then what good company you are in! To die for something that you believe in may be the noblest of actions. Tertullian wrote that "The blood of martyrs is the seed of the Church," which implies that the willing sacrifices of the martyrs' lives led to the conversion of many more. When others see that we are willing to die for our beliefs, they wonder if there's something to it because self-preservation will not allow us to give up our life easily. Only strong faith enables us to willingly die for that belief.

There have been many non-Christians who have died for a cause (kamikazes) or as a result of a demonic lie (jihadists); however, they did not die with joy from the assurance of going to a better place where Jesus is. The early Christian martyrs went to their deaths singing hymns with a joyful countenance. Stephen saw heaven opened up as he was being stoned and was not afraid to die. Recently I saw a photo online of a Christian being placed in a noose by an IS terrorist. He was smiling and waving. If I must die for Jesus, I want to go like that.

I firmly believe that God will give you the courage and strength to bear dying, and that an angel of God is there at the point of death to escort you directly to heaven.

The opposite of fear is not courage—it is faith!

I once heard a story about a Christian church having services in a war-torn country. The parishioners were singing a hymn when gunmen burst through the doors with machine guns. They shouted, "All true believers in Jesus Christ will be shot; all others may leave now." After most of the congregants fled out the doors, the soldiers laid down their arms and said to those remaining, "Brothers and sisters, it's good to be among you—the true Church!"

Check out the Appendix for *Fear Not! Affirmations.* And if you take nothing else from this book, please know that today is the day of salvation. Do not wait another minute to accept Jesus as your Savior (see the *Prayer of Salvation* in the Appendix). Do not, under any condition, accept the mark of the beast or worship his image. Stay strong. Be brave. Think of your reward!

In the meantime, prepare for battle.

Chapter 8
SPIRITUAL WARFARE

*I've never believed in singing about Satan and thinking
he's cool, because he's not.*

DAVE MUSTAINE

There is an invisible world that is just as real as the visible world, and during the Tribulation you will become even more aware of the supernatural. There has been a cosmic conflict between good and evil from the beginning of time, and though our foes are formidable, the victory has already been won through the Cross of Christ. We do not fight for victory but from a position of victory already accomplished.

Cultures have always been fascinated with the supernatural. Literature, television shows, and movies have dealt with the subject and many readers or viewers see the portrayals as fantasy. Others know it as reality because they have had actual experiences with the dark side. There have been so-called satanic strongholds around the world—cities like New Orleans or countries like Uganda. They have greater instances of the occult (haunted houses or demon possession) and evil, such as numerous incidents of murder, mayhem, sin, abuse, depression, drug use, and corrupt rulers. During the Tribulation, the whole world will be the playground of Satan, so you must be on your guard.

Satan is not a metaphor for evil but a powerful angel who committed treason against God and convinced a third of the angels to rebel as well. He seeks to destroy all that is good and, especially, God's people (whether Jews or Christians). *Be sober, be vigilant; because your adversary the devil walks about like a roaring lion, seeking whom he may devour* (1 Peter 5:8).

Ever since his fall, Satan's strategy has been to tempt us with the same agenda that he had, which is to be like God. This is evident from how he tempted Eve in the Garden and culminates when the Antichrist sits in the Temple and declares himself to be god (the abomination of desolation). Evil just seems to be winning—but not really.

Attacks can be physical (illness, inability to breathe, weakness), mental (depression, despair, worry), or spiritual (sin, lack of faith) in nature. Think of the cartoon with the devil sitting on someone's left shoulder and an angel sitting on his right shoulder as they each whispered conflicting suggestions in his ears. The character wouldn't know which one to listen to as they took turns with temptations and encouragements, respectively. Don't listen to your left shoulder! Listen only to God.

Society as a whole—and you as an individual—will be better served to focus on the positive. Philippians 4:8 instructs us to think on things that are true, noble, lovely, pure, and of good report. Let me tell you about God's message to me via an angel. One evening, I was following my family through a restaurant parking lot, feeling very depressed over a matter that actually involved my sin. I was looking down when a man wearing a white three-piece suit (who looked like Kenny Rogers) and standing beside a white Cadillac, looked straight at me and said, "Smile, everything is going to be okay." At first I thought he was being trite, but when I glanced back, he was gone—and so was the Caddy. They just couldn't have moved that fast. I have hung on to that promise whenever times get tough or I feel down. All Christians can hold on to that encouragement because we all have God's promises through His Word.

During the Tribulation, you may have an enlightening dream, or see a vision that focuses you or get encouraged by your own angelic encounter. *"And it shall come to pass in the last days,"* says God, *"that I will pour out My Spirit on all flesh; Your sons and your daughters shall prophesy, your young men shall see visions, your old men shall dream dreams"* (Acts 2:17).

The enemy wants you to hold hatred and unforgiveness in your heart, making you bitter and obnoxious. Develop a tough skin so you are not easily offended by minor irritations. You don't want to put a stumbling block in your own way, having to forgive every perceived slight. Jesus said it would be inevitable that offenses come (Luke 17:1 and Matthew 18:7). If you forgive others, God will forgive you.

It's essential that you and Jesus are "tight." Christianity is not a religion; it's a relationship. Since Satan wants to destroy our witness, our peace, and our lives, we need to stick close to Jesus. Keep your eyes focuses on Him and not the waves. *So Peter went over the side of the boat and walked on the water toward Jesus. But when he saw the strong wind and the waves, he was terrified and began to sink. "Save me, Lord!" he shouted. Jesus immediately reached out and grabbed him. "You have so little faith," Jesus said. "Why did you doubt me?"* Matthew 14:29–31).

Though Satan and his minions are very active and powerful, God has His angelic warriors who will fight for us. In the Old Testament, the prophet Elisha was eluding an evil king seeking to kill him. One morning, Elisha's servant awoke early and saw thousands of the king's horses and warriors ready to pounce on Elisha. The servant alerted his master but Elisha stayed calm, saying, *"Do not fear for those who are with us are more than those who are with them"* (2 Kings 6:16). Elisha's servant thought he had lost his mind since there were only the two of them, until Elisha prayed that his servant's eyes would be opened and there on the hill behind the evil king's armies were thousands of horses and chariots of fire—God's heavenly forces ready to fight for the servants of God.

It is easy to question God's goodness when terrible things are happening all around you, but take heart because we have the means to fight evil and to endure until the finish line. Remember the goal: the Kingdom!

Though we walk in the flesh, we do not war according to the flesh, for the weapons of our warfare are not of the flesh but divinely powerful for the destruction of fortresses. We are destroying speculations and every lofty thing raised up against the knowledge of God and we are taking every thought captive to the obedience of Christ (2 Corinthians 10:3–5 NLT).

DOMINION AND AUTHORITY

I am not talking about Dominion Theology here. Those who believe that Christians will perfect the world before handing it over to Jesus must be clearly delusional due to this world's obvious and continuous degeneration, especially during the Tribulation. Ultimate dominion belongs only to Jesus Christ, the King of the Universe. However, as His children and co-heirs, He has delegated some of that work to us.

Then the kingdom and dominion, and the greatness of the kingdoms under the whole heaven, shall be given to the people, the saints of the Most High. His kingdom is an everlasting kingdom, and all dominions shall serve and obey Him (Daniel 7:27).

When God first created humans, He gave them dominion over the earth. *Then God said, "Let us make human beings in our image, to be like us. They will reign over the fish in the sea, the birds in the sky, the livestock, all the wild animals on the earth, and the small animals that scurry along the ground." So God created human beings in his own image. In the image of God he created them; male and female he created them. Then God blessed them and said, "Be fruitful and multiply. Fill the earth and govern it. Reign over the fish in the sea, the birds in the sky, and all the animals that scurry along the ground"* (Genesis 1:26–28 NLT).

This is called the Cultural Mandate, a Judeo-Christian foundation for all manner of cultural activities: economic engagement, worldly exploration, nature conservation (as well as exploitation), the domestication of animals, and scientific inquiry.

At the fall of man in the Garden of Eden, humans lost many of their privileges along with their immortality. I believe they handed the earth's deed to Satan (See Luke 4:6) until Jesus redeems us, and all of creation, after the Tribulation. However, we are His ambassadors, and He has given us authority in His absence. *Then He called his twelve disciples together and gave them power and authority over all demons, and to cure diseases* (Luke 9:1).

It is not in our own power but in the authority of the name of Jesus that we can call out demons and heal the sick. Stephen the Martyr was not one of the twelve but had power from the Holy Spirit. *And Stephen, full of faith and power, did great wonders and signs among the people (Acts 6:8).* Note: We need to be extra careful about signs and wonders during the Tribulation to be sure we aren't being deceived, but understand that God does not leave us defenseless. *For God has not given us a spirit of fear, but of power and of love and of a sound mind* (2 Timothy 1:7). The same power that raised Jesus from the dead is available to believers who put their trust in Him. Remember there is power in the name of Jesus! Call on Him today.

ARMOR AND WEAPONS

You may not choose to be a warrior in this ultimate battle, but you are, nevertheless. Open warfare is upon us whether we want it or not. Although the victory has already been won by Christ at the Cross, we need to enforce it until He returns to this world and deals with Satan.

Every warrior needs armor and weapons to go into battle. God has provided these for us, but it's up to us to put them on every morning, every night, and any time we feel the attacks of the enemy. Actually, we should be sleeping in our armor!

Finally, my brethren, be strong in the Lord and in the power of His might. Put on the whole armor of God, that you may be able to stand against the wiles of the devil. For we do not wrestle against flesh and blood, but against principalities, against powers, against the rulers of the darkness of this age, against spiritual hosts of wickedness in the heavenly places. Therefore take up the whole armor of God, that you may be able to withstand in the evil day, and having done all, to stand. Stand therefore, having girded your waist with truth, having put on the breastplate of righteousness, and having shod your feet with the preparation of the gospel of peace; above all, taking the shield of faith with which you will be able to quench all the fiery darts of the wicked one. And take the helmet of salvation, and the sword of the Spirit, which is the word of God; praying always (Ephesians 6:10–18).

The first key phrase in the Scripture above is "be strong in the Lord." We do not have the strength to even look the devil in the eye, but it is in and through Jesus that we are strong. When Michael the archangel argued with Satan over Moses' body, he dared not yell at him but said, *"The Lord rebuke you"* (Jude 1:9). There should be a healthy respect for Satan's power, but not fear. It's impossible to read any part of the Bible before coming to a "Fear Not" command from the Lord. *Resist the devil and he will flee from you* (James 4:7).

Now let us briefly examine the armor that we need for spiritual warfare:

• THE BELT OF TRUTH. As the father of lies, Satan deals with confusion and deception. Confront him with the truth and he is gone. There's no better truth than Scripture itself. Know what is true and correct. Be truthful with others, yourself, and especially with God. Honestly confess your sins and your fears to Him.

The Whole Armor of God

• THE BREASTPLATE OF RIGHTEOUSNESS. One of Satan's most successful attacks is accusing us of guilt that we no longer have. He is called the accuser of the brethren in Revelation 12:10, and before he was thrown out of heaven, he stood beside the throne of God pointing out all the sins we committed. That's why it's important to remind him that Jesus paid the sacrifice for our sins, that we are now as white as snow, that God has put our sins as far away as the east is from the west, that we are righteous in Christ. *If I confess my sins, God is faithful and just to forgive my sin and cleanse me from all unrighteousness* (1 John 1:9). Never question your salvation! As a believer, the blood of Jesus covers you, and He gives you His righteousness. The breastplate protects the heart—make sure yours belongs to the Lord.

• SHOES OF THE GOSPEL OF PEACE. As you walk and meet others, it is important to know the Gospel story but also to be at peace with everyone. *Live in peace, and the God of love and peace will be with you (2 Corinthians 13:11b).* Practice mercy and forgiveness and your light will shine in this dark and thankless world. God wants us to live peaceful lives—not fighting with others or being easily offended or judgmental.

Plant your feet and keep your footing and you will stand. *Stand fast therefore in the liberty by which Christ has made us free, and do not be entangled again with a yoke of bondage (Galatians 5:1).* Yes, in war, it is important to stand fast so the enemy doesn't knock you down!

• THE SHIELD OF FAITH can deflect the enemy's arrows and slings—those things that he uses to attack you. Faith is that what you hope for will come to pass. Trust in God's character, His promises, His plan, and His love. David walked onto the battlefield and faced Goliath with the shield of faith. He refused to be intimidated by the giant's taunts and even refused Saul's armor. Instead he defeated the giant with a slingshot and a big confidence in God. Believe that your God is big enough to handle anything that comes your way. Believe His promises of a future full of goodness. Keep your eyes on the prize and just believe!

• THE HELMET OF SALVATION. A helmet protects your mind. *For the weapons of our warfare are not carnal but mighty in God for pulling down strongholds, casting down arguments...bringing every thought into captivity to the obedience of Christ* (2 Corinthians 10:5). Be assured of your salvation. Trust in the shed blood of Jesus to cover your sins. Think clearly and stay sober. It may be tempting to self-medicate in an effort to dull the senses during these difficult times but you need a clear mind to stay focused. Pray, praise, sing, and meditate on Scripture. Give your life to Jesus and die to self. The enemy can threaten all he wants, but it's hard to beat someone who's already dead and you will have boldness when you know that the moment you die, you will be with Jesus.

• THE SWORD OF THE SPIRIT is both a defensive and offensive weapon, and it is the Word of God. You must have Scripture memorized so that it is always at the tip of your tongue. When the devil tempted Jesus in the wilderness, Jesus spoke Scripture back to him, *"It is written...* and the devil departed. Also, know that the Holy Spirit can speak for you. *"But when they arrest you and deliver you up, do not worry beforehand or premeditate what you will speak. But whatever is given you in that hour, speak that; for it is not you who speak, but the Holy Spirit"* (Mark 13:11).

STEPS FOR WINNING THE BATTLE

1. Accept Christ as your personal Savior
2. Repent of sin
3. Put on the whole armor of God

4. Renounce the works of the devil
5. Practice self-control and patience
6. Destroy any occult objects or idols
7. Renew your mind with Scripture
8. Pray with others—pray always!
9. Be thankful
10. Rest in Christ's deliverance
11. Love God with all your heart, mind, and spirit, and love others

But the end of all things is at hand; therefore, be serious and watchful in your prayers (1 Peter 4:7).

SAMPLE PRAYER

"Dear Heavenly Father, I thank you that I am complete in Christ and for your spiritual armor. Spirits are seeking to assault me, and in the blood of Jesus, by His great name and power, I command them to leave me alone. I claim right now that greater is He who is in me than he who is in the world. Lord, please send your angels for a hedge of protection around me. Let evil depart from me and go where Jesus sends it. In Jesus' name, Amen."

Chapter 9
BASIC SURVIVAL STRATEGIES

By perseverance the snail reached the ark.

CHARLES SPURGEON

Throughout history, mankind has had to survive all sorts of circumstances, from extreme weather to miserable oppression, pitiful poverty to world wars. During the Tribulation, anything can happen and probably will. Protecting yourself from these events is not easy and, ultimately, God is in control and we must trust Him for everything. However, some preparation may mean the difference between living another day or not. The Bible says that there are some who will actually survive until the Second Coming, so although it will be hard (and not necessarily the better alternative), it is not impossible. *"And unless those days were shortened, no flesh would be saved; but for the elect's sake those days will be shortened"* (Matthew 24:22).

Chaotic happenings make it almost impossible to guess exactly just what will happen where. A disaster zone is fill-in-the-blank. Living in Florida doesn't preclude an earthquake, and residing in Kentucky doesn't mean you can't get hit with a hurricane. One of the key reasons for the Tribulation is for God to wake up the earth's population before the Book is sealed. Expecting the unexpected rules out any confidence in anyone's ability to save him or her self. We should throw ourselves at the mercy of God.

No matter what time it is or where you are in the world, misery touches all of us at some point, ranging from relatively mild to nearly unbearable. Everybody hurts. Glory hallelujah, all pain and suffering will end when King Jesus reigns!

You may be living in the years just before the Tribulation and notice how the world has gotten progressively worse. Yes, things will only get (much) worse before they get (much) better, so preparation makes good sense. God isn't warning us for His health! Be as prepared as possible before the times grow ever more evil. *But the salvation of the righteous is from the Lord; He is their strength in the time of trouble* (Psalm 37:39).

The following chapters will go into more detail. However, I will begin with a list of essential steps to survive.

PUT ON THE WHOLE ARMOR OF GOD (Ephesians 6:11–17). The belt of Truth, the breastplate of Righteousness, the sandals of the Gospel of Peace, the Shield of Faith, the Helmet of Salvation, and the Sword of the Spirit, which is the Word of God. Before you get dressed in the morning, take a few minutes to mindfully put on your spiritual armor to prepare you for the day and the evil that may come your way.

BE THANKFUL. When you wallow in your misery, depression is hard to beat. Even in the midst of Tribulation, you can still find something to thank God for. *This is the day that the Lord has made, we will rejoice and be glad in it* (Psalm 118:24).

MEMORIZE SCRIPTURE. A Bible may not be available so it's never too soon to commit to memory verses that can deflect the enemy, comfort you, and give you strength to endure tough times. Start with the promises of God. Sing a psalm. Have your testimony and the simple gospel message clear in your mind and always ready to share.

HAVE CLEAN WATER. In your location, have as many sources of water as possible. Streams, ponds, rivers, springs, lakes, as well as cisterns, wells, rain barrels, bottled water, and the city tap. Have on hand purification tablets, chlorine, fire, and a pot for boiling.

KNOW HOW TO START A FIRE. Keep matches and/or lighters dry in water-tight packaging. Learn how to identify flint and starter grasses. Practice lighting a fire.

DOWNSIZE AND SIMPLIFY. Convert any assets you still have to purchase useful commodities that can keep you and/or your family safe, with extra to use as bartering currency and charitable giving. Extricate yourself from the economic system and simplify your life.

Keep an "Exodus" Pack Ready. To grab at a moment's notice, have an easily-toted bag stuffed with the essentials: flint/matches, bottle or canteen of/for water, change of clothes, medicine, Bible, rope, knife, small ax, toilet paper, thin tarp or blanket, granola, bar of soap, towel, alcohol (isopropyl or other!), compass, pen and paper, plastic bags, bandanna, hat, jewelry and/or cash (if still worth anything), photos of loved ones, copies  of important computer files, or documents. See the checklist in the *Appendix*. It looks like a lot, but many items are small.

Stock a Storehouse. If you are in a house or bunker, a pantry is necessary to stockpile whatever you can. It can be for you alone, your family, or even your small community. If possible, keep it stocked with canned meats and vegetables, soups, dried fruits, nuts, jerky, salt, rice, dry beans, sugar, flour, tea, coffee, granola bars, condensed milk, peanut butter, honey, vegetable oil, baby and/or pet food, and water, water, and more water. Pack items in airtight, bug-tight, watertight containers. Add candles, tools, first aid items, needle and thread, duct tape, paper plates and towels, toilet paper, sanitary supplies, bleach, flashlights and batteries, blankets, and tarps.

Consider Moving. It is best at this time to avoid ocean coastlines, the Pacific Rim, all large cities, and obviously, places where the enemy is entrenched and surveillance is omnipresent. A rural area with natural resources and a forest or cave to hide in is ideal, where you can store up provisions, keep the family together, and defend it, if necessary.

Transportation. Consider alternate means of getting around. If gasoline or biofuel are still available, keep your tanks full. You may have or find an older-model car with a simple working engine and no GPS. A small boat is necessary if you live near the water or for use in a flood. Bicycles are great to have around, especially with baskets or trailers. Unless you have your own jet, avoid airplanes, as well as trains and buses. Horses were the primary mode of transportation from creation until the nineteenth century, and they can still do the job. Two pairs of comfortable, closed walking shoes are a must.

KEEP THE LINES OF COMMUNICATION OPEN. Meet with your family, church, and/or community and decide on a plan of action. There's a good possibility that the Internet and cell phones will be down or compromised, so have a specific meeting place near your house and also a contact outside your area. Keep phones charged, have a hand-crank, shortwave or CB radio, smoke signals, handwritten notes, pigeons…prayer.

DEFEND YOURSELF. This is a personal decision and not necessarily a measure of your faith. Jesus told us to turn the other cheek but also to take up our sword. David, a man after God's own heart, used a sling. Elijah, a prophet, had armed men. Angels have flaming swords. It is our instinct to protect and defend those whom we love and the principles that we believe in. The police or military may not be on the side of good and your right to bear arms may be gone. For defense and hunting, I would advise having a gun or rifle. The National Rifle Association suggests a 12-gauge shotgun. Learn how to safely load, shoot, and store (conceal) it. Other weapons such as stun guns, pepper spray, knives, bows and arrows, and martial arts may have limited effect against those who are crazed with wicked intent. However, any weapon is better than none.

STAY WELL. An ounce of prevention is worth a pound of cure. So if at all possible, keep your physical self in good working order. Exercise your body, keep hydrated, always eat when good food is available, try to get enough sleep (in 20-minute naps if you need to be on guard), wash with soap and water daily, take care of any medical conditions, and reduce stress as much as it is possible.

LOVE AND CHARITY. Love is in short supply, but that doesn't change the directive to shine our light in the dark world. The love we show and the peace we project illuminate Jesus. Be generous. Strive to keep in touch with loved ones and assist them the best that you can. Hopefully, you are with your family or a community of believers who can share work and necessities, encourage you when you lose hope, nurse you when you're sick, and pray for you. It's been said that home is where the heart is. If you've had to leave your home or are wandering homeless or alone, don't forget that Jesus has prepared a mansion just for you with the family of God.

Chapter 10
PRACTICAL CONCERNS

Common sense is the best sense I know of.

LORD CHESTERFIELD

The modern conveniences of the twenty-first century have made it harder to live the simple life, but to survive, we must learn how to exist without electricity and provisions supplied by government or companies. When we turn on the faucet, we expect clean water to pour out of the tap, in the precise temperature we desire. Supermarkets and restaurants provide food without our ever having to touch a live animal or till the ground. Homes are bought without the buyer ever lifting a hammer. Computers and televisions provide entertainment, information, and relationship without having to experience a live human being.

To survive in hard times, we need to be self-sufficient and knowledgeable of some basic skills.

WATER

Our bodies need water to survive. We can go without food for a month depending on body type, but we can't go more than three days without water. The minimum drinking water supply is one gallon per person per day. During the Tribulation, food and clean water are scarce, so fill up with clean water at every opportunity.

Surface water may be obtained from rivers, ponds, lakes, or streams. It is usually easy to find but prone to contamination from viruses, bacteria, parasites, chemicals, or radiation. Water should always be purified before consuming. Birds frequently fly toward water at dawn and dusk in a direct, low path. Insects and frogs are good indicators that water is nearby. Grazing mammals usually head to water twice a day. Green vegetation at the base of a cliff or mountain may indicate a natural spring, and valleys or low-lying drainage areas may hold moisture. However, the lower the elevation or further from the source of water, the greater the possibility of contamination. Avoid water that is dark, contains floating material or is near where defecation takes place.

Ground water is found under the earth's surface and is naturally filtered as it moves through the ground and into underground aquifers. To create a well, dig a three-foot wide hole about ten feet from your water source. Dig until water begins to seep in and then dig about another foot. Line the sides of your hole with wood or rocks so that no more mud will fall in. Let it sit overnight so the dirt and sand will settle. When close to shore, dig a similarly described hole one dune inland.

Naturally clean water may be obtained from the source of a spring or at the very top of a mountain stream. Rainwater is usually clean as well. Collect rainwater in nonporous containers; snow provides an excellent source of water, but always melt it first before consuming.

You can usually eke out some moisture from plants and other vegetation, either from hollow portions of the plant or by collecting condensation from a solar still. Tie off a clear plastic bag with green plant material inside, leaving an empty corner at the bottom and placed in direct sunlight. A cup of water should appear by day's end. Be sure to drink it before sunset when the plant will reabsorb the moisture. You can make a water bottle from the stomach of a large animal. Thoroughly flush out the stomach with water and tie off the bottom. Never drink blood, saltwater, or urine.

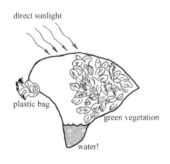

direct sunlight

plastic bag

green vegetation

water!

Without an elaborate purification system, there are a couple of basic ways to purify water. Sediment can be filtered through cloth. Boiling will kill most organisms and is the most readily available, needing just a fire and a pot. Once the water comes to a boil, continue boiling for at least one full minute (three minutes in high altitudes). You will lose some volume so start with more than you'll need. If it tastes too flat, add oxygen by pouring it back and forth between two clean containers, or add a pinch of salt.

When unable to boil your water, you can use chlorine or iodine. Mix eight to ten drops of plain household chlorine bleach per gallon (two drops per liter)—double that amount if the water remains cloudy. You can also use iodine tincture from a first-aid kit—add five to six drops per quart or liter. Mix the solution thoroughly and let stand for about thirty minutes.

Distilling water removes the most impurities and can be used for salt water if no de-salting tablets are available. Distillation involves boiling water and then collecting the vapor that condenses back into liquid. To distill, fill a pot halfway with water. Tie a cup to the handle on the pot's lid so that the cup will hang right-side-up when the lid is upside-down, making sure the cup is not touching the water. Boil the water for ten minutes. The water that drips from the lid into the cup is distilled. Sip water instead of guzzling it and, if water is scarce, do not eat solid food, as it requires water for digestion.

FOOD

Because you sinned, I have placed a curse on the ground. All your life you will struggle to scratch a living from it. It will grow thorns and thistles for you, though you will eat of its grains. All your life you will sweat to produce food until your dying day (Genesis 3:17–19 NLT). This struggle for food is a daily battle during the Tribulation, made more so from drought, bugs, disease, disasters, economic situations, pollution, scarcity, contamination, blockades, and economic conditions.

God provided manna for the wandering Israelites, Jesus fed five thousand people with two fish and five loaves of bread, He provides for the birds of the air, and He can supply your needs as well. *"Look at the birds of the air, for they neither sow nor reap nor gather into barns; yet your heavenly Father feeds them. Are you not of more value than they?"* (Matthew 6:26).

Getting adequate nutrition is important to stay sharp and focused for the hard work of surviving in the Tribulation. The ideal diet contains all five kinds of nutrients: carbohydrates, fats, protein, vitamins, and minerals. These are obtained from five groups of foods: meat, dairy, fruits/vegetables, grains, and fats.

Stock up on nonperishables, stored in tightly covered containers, in a cool, dry spot away from toxins. Bulk quantities of beans, rice, flour, salt, oil, powdered milk, peanut butter, corn, jams, bullion, and tea can last almost indefinitely if stored properly. My husband is fond of telling me that honey is the only food that never spoils—we have more jars than we'll ever use in our cupboard! Jerky is light and easily transported. Canned meats, soups, and vegetables can add variety. Make sure to have a manual can opener.

Bread is the most basic food, made from just flour, water, and a pinch of salt, and can be baked in whatever is available. Adding baking powder or yeast will make the bread rise and various ingredients will enhance the flavor.

STANDARD BISCUIT RECIPE

Ingredients:

2 cups flour

1/2 teaspoon salt

3 teaspoons baking powder

3–4 tablespoons shortening (butter, oil or lard)

3/4 cup milk

1. Preheat oven to 425°.
2. In bowl, combine dry ingredients.
3. Cut in shortening until crumbly.
4. Add milk. Stir gently until dough holds together.
5. Gather into ball and knead gently with floured fingers.
6. Roll or press out dough 1/2 inch thick. Cut in circles.
7. Arrange an inch apart and bake in hot oven for 12–15 minutes.

If you end up on the run or exhaust your supplies, it's time to hunt and forage.

You can, with relatively few exceptions, eat anything that swims, walks, or flies. Avoid scavengers. Watch what mammals are eating, but don't depend on the birds as many of them have special resistance to toxins.

Mammals are excellent sources of protein and tasty, too. This is where your rifle or bow will come in handy, or you can set a trap or snare to catch smaller mammals. If possible, keep all animals alive until ready to cook and then kill as humanely as possible. You can boil for tenderness, bake in a hole covered with hot rocks, or roast by suspending meat over a fire.

To clean small game, you will need a sharp pocketknife. Start by pinching the animal's loose skin behind the top of its neck or in the middle of its back. When you have the skin pinched in one hand, use the other to cut around the neck and around the tail. Then grab the skin with one hand on either side of the incision and pull in opposite directions toward the head and neck. The skin will peel off easily.

After eating your fill, preserve what is left over by drying in the sun or smoking the meat to create a jerky. To dry, hang long, thin strips in the sun away from other animals' reach. Depending on the humidity and temperature, it may take a few days to dry. You'll know it's done when the meat is dark and dry.

All species of birds are edible and nesting birds present eggs. Always leave at least two eggs behind and mark them if you intend to raid the same nest again, leaving the marked eggs every time. Worms can be eaten and will be better if soaked in water for a few minutes. Dig in damp soil or look on the ground after it rains. Grubs and other insect larvae are also good to eat if you can stomach them. Fish is an excellent source of protein, and although there are just a few saltwater species that are poisonous, all freshwater fish is safe to eat as long as the source is relatively clean.

Plants are good sources of food because they are widely available, easily obtained and can meet your nutritional needs in the right combinations. The critical factor in using plants is to avoid accidental poisoning. Eat only those plants that you know are safe to eat, and in lieu of such knowledge, you can use the Universal Edibility Test.

UNIVERSAL EDIBILITY TEST

1. Test only one part of a potential food plant at a time.
2. Separate the plant into its basic components—leaves, stems, roots, buds, and flowers.
3. Smell for strong or acid odors.
4. Do not eat for 8 hours before starting the test.

5. During fasting, test for contact poisoning by placing a piece of the plant inside your elbow for 15 minutes.

6. Drink only clean water and the plant you are testing.

7. Select a small portion of a single part and prepare it the way you plan to eat it.

8. Touch a small portion to the outer surface of your lips.

9. If after 3 minutes there is no reaction, place the plant part on your tongue, hold for 15 minutes.

10. If there is no reaction, chew a pinch and hold it in your mouth for 15 minutes. Do not swallow.

11. If no burning, itching, numbing, stinging or other irritation occurs, then swallow the food.

12. Wait 8 hours. If any ill effects occur, induce vomiting and drink a lot of water.

13. If no ill effects occur, eat another portion. If no ill effects occur, the plant part as prepared is safe for eating.

Avoid plants that can be toxic such as those growing along the side of the road, lawns that have been treated with pesticide, at the bottom of runoff, or in dumps and industrial areas.

The inner bark of a tree, between the outer layer and the wood, may be eaten raw or cooked, or pounded into flour. Native Americans included bark as an important part of their diet, and a tribe in upstate New York, called Adirondack, means "bark eaters." Evergreen trees are mostly edible and offer a good inner bark and needles that can be boiled into a tea (not to mention they make comfy bedding). Pine nuts are delicious and healthful. Pine stumps and roots, when extracted by heat and pressure, produce pine tar, which is useful for skin ailments, hoof salve, soap-making, and as a roofing material.

In general, berries are easy to find and pick. Aggregate berries, such as raspberries and blackberries, are 99 percent edible. Purple, blue and black berries are 90 percent edible. Red berries are a risky 50 percent edible. And green, yellow or white berries are only 10 percent edible.

The common dandelion is readily found and familiar to most, popping up in flowerbeds, lawns, pastures, meadows, and other moist, open spaces. The entire plant is edible and the tender young leaves in spring make a great salad or boiled in a soup. Seaweed is full of vitamins. Mushrooms are risky unless you can positively identify them. If available, a field guide would make a great addition to your pack.

Dandelion – all parts are edible

Most food can be preserved by being packed in salt, smoked over a fire, dried in the sun, properly canned, kept cold in snow, or in a refrigerator/ freezer if electricity is working.

MAKING FIRE

Fire provides heat, light, a means of signaling, a source for cooking food and purifying water, to dry clothes, and affords protection from wild animals. Fire also provides comfort and relaxation.

Ideally, you will have a lighter or some dry matches. Available in camping supply stores is a match with hand-dipped, varnished heads that will light in wind or when wet and burns 12 seconds—enough time to light most fires. A metal match is an artificial flint. When stroked with an object, the friction creates a spark that can be used to light tinder. Flint and steel are effective for starting fires but the necessary materials may be hard to find. Some flint options include iron pyrite, agate, or jasper. Any steel can be used, such as a file or knife.

A fire needs something to burn in three stages—tinder, kindling, and fuel. Tinder is dry material that ignites with just a spark, such as shredded inner bark, dead ferns or moss, straw, sawdust, dead evergreen needles, lint from pockets or seams, down feathers, seed heads, rotted wood, steel wool, a pinch of gunpowder, or a battery. Kindling is readily combustible material that you add to the burning tinder. Dry kindling increases the fire's temperature so that it will ignite less combustible material. Sources of kindling are small twigs, heavy cardboard or wood that has been doused in oil or wax. Fuel is less combustible material that burns slowly and steadily once ignited, such as dry wood, dry grasses twisted into bunches, dried animal dung, coal, oil, wax, or peat. The fire triangle is heat, fuel, and oxygen—all three need to be present for a fire to continue burning.

To build a fire, find a spot that is dry, protected from wind, suitably placed in relation to your fuel supply and shelter, if applicable. Clear a large circle so you stay in control. If time allows, construct a firewall with rocks, bricks, or logs to direct the heat where you want it, reduce flying sparks and block some wind. The fire needs oxygen to burn, so allow air to circulate under and around it. Avoid using wet or porous rocks as they may explode when heated. Of course, a small barbecue or fire pan would work.

The direct spark method is the easiest of the primitive methods to use, and the flint and steel method is the most reliable. Strike a flint or other hard, sharp-edged rock with a piece of carbon steel. With a little patience and practice, a spark will be produced. When a spark has caught in the tinder, blow on it (this is where the oxygen comes in). The spark will spread into a flame. Keep it going by adding fuel. Before leaving the area, be sure the fire is completely extinguished and all traces of human activity are erased.

When you need a smaller or portable fire, create a lamp or torch. You need to render animal fat into tallow by cooking it over a low temperature until melted. Remove any particles by straining the liquid through a porous cloth. If not for immediate use, fill a clean jar, cover and store in a cool, dark place. Tallow can be used as a lubricant, to make soap, and as fuel for a lamp or torch. Cattails make excellent torches with a built-in handle; cut three feet, dip the head in tallow, and light. The bark of a birch tree burns when wet—put strips of bark in a hole cut into a branch or sapling and replace as the bark strips burn out.

To put out a fire, throw water or soil on it. For a grease fire, put a lid on it or smother with baking soda (you'll need lots!). If on a person, stop–drop–and roll.

SHELTER

Deciding what kind of shelter to build depends on the environment (both physical and political), available materials, how much time you have to build it, and how long you plan to be habitating there. A good shelter should provide protection from the elements and concealment from enemy observation.

Some considerations for the placement of your shelter include:

- Availability of building materials
- Source of natural water
- Level space on higher ground
- Away from insects, poisonous plants, dead trees, large animal trails, falling rocks, or rushing water
- Camouflaged escape route
- Position doorway so it's facing east

There are many designs of shelters, from living in a cave with a fire at the entrance to modern mansions with the latest conveniences. However, if you are homeless or starting a camp in the wilderness, a well-designed natural shelter needs to start with the framework.

First, you need a ridgepole, which will be the main beam that will support the roof and walls. It needs to be sturdy, de-stubbed, about the diameter of your wrist and long enough to create the desired shelter size, at least ten feet in length. You can easily construct an A-frame or lean-to by laying the ridgepole into a support tree and hanging a tarp over the pole or using smaller support poles as a base for boughs or sod. If you need to lash poles together, use rope or plant material. For other emergency shelters, consider caves, rock outcroppings, trees with low branches, formed ice or snow, a raised platform, mud hut, sod, or tepee if you have a tarp. Insulate as best you can.

Basic A-frame Shelter
Add tarp, branches, snow, etc.

Designate a latrine in a shady spot far enough away from your immediate shelter and any water source but not so far as to be inconvenient. Cover urine and/or feces with dirt and turn often.

Hang food off the ground out of the reach of small mammals. Keep your shelter and surrounding area clean and tidy.

For long-term shelter in a cold or temperate climate, a log cabin makes a great house. The logs provide a stable and insulated structure for excellent protection. When selecting logs, make sure they are manageable. Gather fourteen eight-to-ten-foot-long strong poles. At each of the four corners of the house, bury three of the poles 8–12 inches into the ground in a triangular shape and tap dirt around them to hold them in place. Two feet to the left of the front right corner, place two more poles, which will make the doorway. Once all of the support poles are in place, stack logs between them. A straw-and-mud mortar can be made by thoroughly mixing an equal amount of mud with fibrous material like dry grass, straw, or ferns. Pack the gaps between logs and when dry, the mixture will form a hard bond to keep the structure together and provide insulation. Construct a roof by placing logs side by side until it is covered. Fill with mortar and cover with boughs. Make sure you leave an adequate ventilation hole that can be opened and closed for a fire (and for stargazing).

NAVIGATION

A compass can be of tremendous value when outside of your comfort zone. Before setting off, determine a landmark and its compass bearing so you have a point of reference. If you have to navigate around an obstruction, keep a sight line to a large object in the distance so you can stay focused on your general course. It's a basic fact that the sun rises in the east and sets in the west.

The North Star has been used as a guiding star for thousands of years and is a reference point for navigators and astronomers. Through observation and experience, travelers and scientists discovered that the North Star lights the way to true north. Knowing how to find it in the northern hemisphere is one of the most basic survival skills. (The Southern Cross assists those in the southern hemisphere.)

The northern axis of the earth points directly toward the North Star. Unlike a magnetic compass, the star always points to true north as there is no magnetic declination to deal with. The North Star is also called Polaris because when you are observing this star, you are facing toward the North Pole. Then west would be to your left, east to your right, and south behind you.

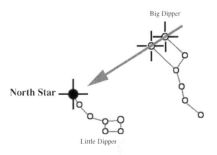

Though clearly visible on a clear night, the North Star is not the brightest star in the sky. It is about average when compared to other stars. The key to locating it is to first find the Big Dipper, a group of stars in a constellation known as Ursa Major (Great Bear) just north of the celestial pole. The second key is to find the similarly shaped constellation of stars known as the Little Dipper, also known as Ursa Minor. It's a little harder to find but, fortunately, its big brother points the way. The star we are seeking is the brightest of the Little Dipper stars and located at the tip of the dipper's handle.

Directions to finding the North Star:

- Locate the Big Dipper in the northern sky. It's identifiable by its large size and distinct shape.
- Locate the two stars that form the outer edge (see diagram).
- Draw an imaginary line straight through the two stars of the dipper edge and toward the Little Dipper. The line will point very close to the handle of the Little Dipper.
- The brightest star in the Little Dipper is at the end of its handle. This is the North Star.

When you have found the North Star, you can also use it to determine your latitude north of the equator by measuring the angle formed between the horizon and the star. *"He comes from the north as golden splendor; with God is awesome majesty"* (Job 37:22). Also see Isaiah 14:13. Is heaven in the direction of far north? Hmm.

PETS AND LIVESTOCK

Animals were created by God to assist us, feed us, and comfort us. They are part of the so-called cycle of life that keeps the planet healthy. Dogs make great companions and guards. Cats kill vermin. Birds warn of biological warfare and can uplift with a song. It seems that animals have an innate sense of impending natural disasters, running for the hills before people even have a clue.

During the Tribulation, animals also struggle with horrors and trials.

Pets that have been left behind by the Rapture may be wandering around scared and hungry, too domesticated to fend for themselves. I prefer the thought that God, in His mercy, gently puts them to sleep! If you have a pet, be sure that it has an identifying tag in case it gets lost. Pets today usually have microchips but these need a scanner to retrieve the information, and frankly, scanners are to be avoided.

Tropical fish are too fragile for the Tribulation environment and personal aquariums are a luxury that's no longer sensible. Set Nemo free.

Livestock provides nutritious food and a means to make a living. Just a few laying hens can supply eggs for your family with leftovers for bartering. Add a rooster and you'll reproduce chickens for an occasional dinner or trade. A cow or goat can provide milk, butter, and cheese. Sheep provide wool for yarn. Horses are great for transportation, companionship, herding, and plowing the field. Every animal should have its own stall in a barn with doors and windows that can be closed up against the elements and biological, chemical, or atomic attacks. However, in severe weather conditions when you can't depend on the structure for protection, whether floods, tornadoes, or fire, it's best to allow the animals a way of escape. They may barge down the gates anyway.

God has put us in charge of the animals, and it is our responsibility to treat them with kindness. Domesticated pets and farm animals depend on us for their food and safety. Abuse should never be tolerated and neglect should not be an option. Be sure to ask God's blessings on your animals.

RATION, BARTER, STOCKPILE, AND SHARE

There is a difference between hoarding and stockpiling. To hoard implies greedily grabbing everything without considering the needs of others, and usually for no other reason than from fear or selfishness. Stockpiling is a systematic gathering of goods to sustain you and your family through the lean years.

God revealed to Joseph that there would be seven years of plenty followed by seven years of famine. This is what Joseph told Pharaoh, *"Let Pharaoh appoint officials over the land and let them collect one-fifth of all the crops during the seven good years. Have them gather all the food and grain of these good years into the royal storehouses, and store it away so there will be food in the cities. That way there will be enough to eat when the seven years of famine come"* (Genesis 41:34–36 NLT).

If you are living in a house, it is important to collect goods as you can acquire them. Not useless collectibles like baseball cards and porcelain dolls, or electronic gadgets and knick-knacks, but practical items and food. As previously mentioned, things to stock up on include blankets, toilet paper, medicine, coffee, tea, salt, rice, flour, canned goods, honey, peanut butter, warm clothes, powdered milk, and whatever else can be used to trade.

In times of plenty, consumption is not an issue and in fact, can become a problem by creating a materialistic society, pollution, entitlement complexes, and economic collapse. However, during tough times, it is best to ration food, water, and fuel. A few bites of a simple meal can sustain you until the next mealtime. If hunger pangs strike, a handful of trail mix, a piece of fruit or bread and butter will quiet the stomach rumblings and keep up your energy. Don't guzzle water but swish around your mouth before swallowing. Each person should use at least one gallon of water per day, for drinking, as well as cooking and body washing. Fuel should be used only when necessary.

Bartering is an important means of acquiring goods and services in a cashless society, and without accepting the mark of the beast, it's impossible to buy or sell. Your only way of acquiring goods is to trade for them, or utilizing a type of community currency. *He required everyone—great and small, rich and poor, slave and free—to be given a mark on the right hand or on the forehead. And no one could buy or sell anything without that mark, which was either the name of the beast or the number representing his name* (Revelation 13:16–17 NLT).

It won't be easy to resist the mark when you have children depending on you for food or medicine. Without the mark, groceries are unattainable and you can't buy fuel. No online banking, Internet commerce, or electronic fund transfers. Certainly, paying the bills would be a challenge. Instead, you'll need to trade for necessary services or items. Remember that, with faith, God will provide for your needs.

Bartering has a long and necessary history. The things of value now are water, food, blankets, tools, fuel, medicine, clothing, and shoes. Any practical item can be traded for something that you need but don't have. The equality of the value in a one-on-one barter can be an issue so negotiate and compromise calmly. Keep in mind conversations about what other people may need and then barter accordingly.

Services can also be bartered. A plumber does repair work for a dentist who fixes his teeth. Any skill can be exchanged for another: carpenters, plumbers, tailors, musicians, nurses, laborers, blacksmiths, farmers, millers, cobblers, bakers, and others have valuable talents and abilities that can be bartered, contributing to your community or for helping out someone less fortunate.

The greatest commodities are love, faith, mercy, kindness, loyalty, and hope. Jesus gives us all of these great things abundantly and so commands us to share what we have with our sisters and brothers. That doesn't mean that you should give away every possession you have (although there are those who are called for that), but after your family is provided for, you share with other believers. God loves a cheerful giver and will bless you if you are generous. *"Give, and it will be given to you: good measure, pressed down, shaken together and running over"* (Luke 6:38).

MAKING A LIVING

In the early part of the Tribulation working for a living may continue pretty much as always. Electronic fund transfers already replace an actual paycheck.

Identification numbers or cards with chips are issued to keep track of you and your money.

After the Antichrist comes to power and his economic system is implemented, if you do not take the mark (and my friend, I hope you don't), then it will be impossible for you to work a "real" job. An employer cannot pay you without scanning your chip/tattoo, and you can't log in to your timesheet. No more being paid under the table with cash. You aren't able to use the banks. And even gold, silver, and precious gems will be worthless. *"They will throw their silver into the streets, and their gold will be like refuse; their silver and their gold will not be able to deliver them in the day of the wrath of the Lord"* (Ezekiel 7:19).

This is when bartering your skills and services come into play. Learn a trade, or perfect an old one. Carpenter, fisherman, doctor, midwife, seamstress, farrier, musician, innkeeper, mechanic, herbalist, preacher, blacksmith, baker, builder, plumber—if you have a skill or service to offer, and are fair, amiable and competent, word will get around.

Working for room and board can be a good arrangement if the situation is right. Caretaker, nanny, farmer, maid, nurse, and personal assistant are some possibilities. Any talent that you possess can and should be used for the glory of God, which in turn, will bless you. Just making it through the day is making a living during the Tribulation.

DE-STRESSING TECHNIQUES

Stress can come from any situation or thought that makes you feel frustrated, angry, or anxious. To say that the Tribulation is a stressful time is an understatement. Facing evil on a daily basis, trying to scratch out a living, and looking forward to probable martyrdom is not exactly conducive to a calm and peaceful life. Although those who continue to reject God may think they are buying time or stability, they are in a most precarious place as His wrath pours down on the earth. *"...men's hearts failing them from fear and the expectation of those things which are coming on the earth, for the powers of the heavens will be shaken"* (Luke 21:26).

This world has been increasingly stressing us out since the fall of humankind, having to deal with the curse daily. Although good stress can motivate us to action in threatening situations, persistent or chronic stress is harmful to our bodies, causing abdominal pain, heart disease, increased risk of infections and depression, just to name a few. The following are some strategies for coping with stress.

✔ GET IN TOUCH WITH NATURE

Granted, being outdoors may not be an option due to natural or man-made disasters, or if you need to avoid detection. But if there is a local park in your town or wilderness around your rural property, or even an arboretum, communing with the trees and feeling the grass under bare feet can ground you in a way that is very basic. The naturalist John Muir said, "Come to the woods, for here is rest." [1]

Just gazing at a tranquil (not stagnant!) lake or a running stream brings a peaceful feeling. Stroll on the beach, slide on some snow, contemplate the stars, hug a tree, laugh at the squirrels, marvel at the colors of a sunset or the deep blue of the daytime sky.

Domesticated animals are wonderful de-stressors because they are cute and simple—innocent casualties in mankind's struggle. Pets are extra special because they form a bond with us, and a cheery bird, a devoted dog, or a precocious cat can refresh our souls. It's been found that just stroking your pet will lower your blood pressure!

✔ MUSIC

There have been reports that heaven is filled with the most glorious sounds, so no wonder it is soothing to hear angelic choirs with multiple harmonies accompanied by stringed instruments. In times of trouble you may just want to sing the blues, or satisfy your pain with the mournful tones of a bagpipe, or the rage of heavy metal. Music affects our emotions on a subconscious level so if you have a choice, choose tunes and instruments that are uplifting. Golden oldies can bring you back to the good old days for a short respite. Wind chimes and nature sounds soothe and calm your soul.

If you have natural talent as a musician, your particular instrument could be part of an exodus pack. With just one acoustic guitar and a few memorized songs and hymns, you can lift the spirits of a whole assembly or your small group. A harmonica is easy to learn and easy to carry. Anyone can make music with a drum or kazoo. Use your voice—hum if that's all you have!

David was called to play music for Saul to ease his depression. *Let us find a good musician to play the harp for you whenever the tormenting spirit is bothering you. The harp music will quiet you, and you will soon be well again* (1 Samuel 16:16).

A companion to music, dance can help you express your feelings. Dance movement, like exercise, allows the physical release of the stress and adrenaline in your body. You can praise God with the body He gave you with some worship dancing. *And David danced before the Lord with all his might* (2 Samuel 6:14).

✔ ART OR HOBBIES

Everyone has at least one activity that seems to make time fly when engrossed in it. That's why those kinds of activities are called pastimes, and far better than mere amusements. I suspect that art and hobby supplies, free time, and the ability to do as one pleases are at a premium. However, expressing your pent-up concerns in a creative way is a great outlet for your stress and a familiar pastime can be a great comfort.

If you are without paints, draw in the dirt or put pencil to paper. Photograph loved ones or document the strange happenings around you. Sew, woodwork, sculpt—art media is really endless so do whatever you enjoy with whatever supplies are available. In so doing, you can bless others with your creations.

✔ AROMATHERAPY

Odors are all around us, from our own bodies to the food we put in them, from the grass under our feet to scented candles, from a rose bush to a wet dog. Throughout history, woods and spices have been burned as incense to represent the prayers of the people rising up to heaven. Certain scents can trigger memories and emotions, and pleasing fragrances can lighten our mood. Our sense of smell is usually keen. Everyone has their own favorite scents and most would scrunch up their face when the nose catches a malodorous whiff.

Essential oils stimulate the brain to trigger a reaction and, when inhaled into the lungs, the naturally occurring chemicals supply therapeutic benefits. Diffusing eucalyptus essential oil to help ease congestion is an example, but some essential oils can be dangerous if not used correctly. Moderation is key to not "burn out" the senses. Alternative sources of aromatherapy include soaps, candles, incense, herbs, perfume, flowers, cooking, new-mown grass, baby's breath, clean bed sheets, your lover's pheromones, the ocean, a damp forest …

Some aromas are best for relaxation and lifting spirits, including jasmine, lavender, chamomile, and rosemary.

✔ EXERCISE

Light exercise is one of the most important stress-busters. You get a sense of wellbeing just by moving your body. Knowing that you are doing something good for yourself can lift depression, plus it helps to release the pent-up emotions and adrenaline that has you all pumped up. It's best to avoid very strenuous exercise at this time—no extreme sports! You don't want to hurt yourself or create more stress on your body. Go for a walk, run, throw a ball, swim, or, as mentioned earlier, dance. If you're stuck inside without resources, there's always calisthenics. Touch your toes, rotate your neck, do leg lifts, sit-ups, push-ups, jumping jacks and knee bends. Make sure to stretch, stay strong, and in shape.

✔ DEEP BREATHING

Deep breathing is exactly what it sounds like—allowing yourself to breathe slowly and deeply to reduce tension and create relaxation. You can do the following exercise whenever you have a few spare moments. Sit in a comfortable position. Place your right hand on your chest and your left hand on your abdomen. Inhale slowly and deeply through your nose and into your abdomen, letting your left hand rise up as much as feels comfortable. Slowly count to four as you inhale. Now breathe out through your mouth, pursing your lips slightly and making a quiet whooshing sound. Count slowly to four while you exhale. Continue to breathe slowly and deeply, focusing on your relaxation, until you have taken at least ten deep breaths.

✔ ADDITIONAL RELAXATION TECHNIQUES
- Pray, pray, and pray some more
- Repeat the promises of God
- Get enough sleep
- Allow extra time to get things done and to travel where you're going
- Pace yourself
- Simplify; be organized
- Lay your burdens down at the Cross
- Respect your limitations
- Live in the moment; one day at a time
- Take a warm bath or shower
- Spend time with a friend or family member
- Write your thoughts and fears in a journal
- Talk less; listen more (loose lips sink ships!)
- Be kind to unkind people
- Allow for interruptions or divine appointments
- Count your blessings, small as they may be
- Gather with other believers
- Visualize a favorite place or scenario
- Read the "Fear Not Affirmations" in the Appendix
- Remind yourself that God is in control!

In God I have put my trust; I will not be afraid. What can man do to me? (Psalm 56:11).

Chapter 11
NATURAL CATASTROPHES

There is no security on this earth; there is only opportunity.

GENERAL DOUGLAS MACARTHUR

The Tribulation is a time of unprecedented natural phenomena and, unfortunately, most of it is catastrophic. As the birth of the Kingdom draws near, the frequency and intensity of the occurrences increase. *"And there will be famines, pestilences, and earthquakes in various places. All these are the beginning of sorrows* (Matthew 24:7–8). We've seen floods where they've never happened before and new flood events that are deemed the worst in history—of biblical proportions. The news is getting progressively worse all over the globe.

During the Tribulation, natural catastrophes become the mighty manifestations of God. There's nothing like a tornado reducing everything you own to little bits to get your attention. The less our world wants to hear God's voice, the louder the elements will shout.

Earthquakes, volcanoes, and floods have been around for a long time, carving up planet Earth to the landscape we see today. Scientists have mapped the fault lines and the ring of fire, but from what we know about God, anything can happen—and probably does during the Tribulation. In fact, all of the events culminate with the mother of all earthquakes as Jesus' feet touch down on the Mount of Olives.

There are some basic preparedness actions that are the same for every disaster and include: (1) a plan, (2) an exodus pack, and most importantly, (3) the whole armor of God. However, there are some specific things that you can do to protect yourself during each of the following natural catastrophes.

EARTHQUAKES

An earthquake is a sudden and rapid shaking of the earth caused by shifting rock beneath the earth's surface. Huge tectonic plates that form the earth's crust move over, under, and past each other, resulting in shaking that can cause buildings and bridges to collapse, the disruption of utility services, and triggering mudslides or tsunamis. Cities in earthquake-prone zones have strong building requirements and many buildings can survive a small earthquake; however, anything over 6.0 on the Richter scale will cause major collapses. Although it can be determined if a certain area is prone to earthquakes, the timing is hard to predict and the Bible talks about diverse places. Sometimes smaller tremors herald something larger to come. There is a strong possibility that you will experience an earthquake during the Tribulation period.

Earthquake Survival Tips

Fleeing animals are a good clue of an impending earthquake, but you have to be alert and ready. When the ground starts rolling, quickly go outside the building if you are on flat, open land, and move away from all buildings, power lines, and streetlights. If you are in a large public building, step to a clear area away from windows and fixtures, but don't try to leave as it will take too long and debris will be falling. Go under a strong desk or doorframe and cover your head. A cell phone can be a lifesaver, that is, if it continues to work. Whistle (or keep one with you) to alert rescue personnel that you are trapped. In your home, you can keep property damage to a minimum and protect yourself by thinking ahead. Bolt heavy furniture to wall studs, store heavy, breakable or flammable items in low, closed cabinets with latches. Brace overhead fixtures, secure electronics, and install flexible pipe fittings to avoid gas or water leaks. After an earthquake, evaluate the damage, turn off utilities, and check on your neighbors. Try not to panic and realize that God is in control!

VOLCANOES

A volcano is an opening in the earth's surface, usually atop a mountain but sometimes under the ocean. There are also hot spring areas with bubbling, steaming, scalding water that's been heated from the earth's interior and has the potential to explode in a large-area, volcanic-type eruption. Sulfuric hot springs and sinkholes can collapse and swallow anything above them. A super volcano has a large caldera and the potential to cause widespread devastation if it blows. Yellowstone National Park is an example.

When pressure builds up, a volcano will erupt, pushing gases and molten rock up and out of the hole. Lava and ash are byproducts that can be deadly, although in their cooled state become the raw materials for industrial and chemical uses. The good thing about volcanoes is geologists know where they are located, mostly dotted on the so-called Ring of Fire, so it just seems smart to avoid them and the twenty-mile danger area around them.

Volcano Survival Tips

With volcanoes, there is usually some kind of warning so that you have time to evacuate the area before it blows. Signals of imminent activity are rumblings, earthquakes, steam or gas clouds, and fleeing animals. Lava consumes everything in its path. Since it flows with the help of gravity, run at a right angle to the lava flow, to the side and not down in front of it. The chances of humans outrunning lava or a pyroclastic flow are slim. Climbing a tree or structure is futile as it will just burn and collapse under the molten lava. Cover yourself with water if available to protect from burns and place a damp cloth over your mouth to protect from toxic fumes.

If you are not in the direct path of lava flow or in an evacuation area, stay in your house. Rock debris and ash is a big concern so close all windows, doors, and dampers; bring animals into a closed shelter; cover water storage areas and machinery; wear long-sleeved shirts and pants; use a dust mask or damp bandanna to help you breathe. Avoid low-lying areas where gases can collect and mudflows can smother. Afterward, stay off the ash on the ground, clear roofs from ash-fall, and assist your neighbors.

FLOODS

Flooding can happen anywhere and low-lying areas are particularly at risk. Raging rivers, rising creeks, bursting levees, and storm surges from an over-abundance of rainfall from hurricanes or other weather systems can knock down big trees and houses, carrying everything with it in a roiling, traveling stew. An overabundance of rain can cause mudslides; dam failure can be catastrophic for whole towns due to its dumping of a large amount of water in a short time. Seismic activity can produce tsunamis—gigantic waves that have the power to wipe out thousands of people living near a coastline. Standing water is detrimental to animals, rotting hooves and carrying their waste. Flooding damages or destroys structures, furnishings, and transportation.

We have the promise of God that no matter how much it rains, He will never destroy the earth again by flooding and the sign of that covenant is the rainbow. *"Never again will there be a flood that will destroy all life. When I see the rainbow in the clouds, I will remember the eternal covenant between God and every living creature on earth"* (Genesis 9:16 NLT).

Flood Survival Tips

It is important that you know how to swim, or at the very least, to tread water or "doggy paddle" to stay afloat. Keep important documents or belongings in sealed plastic bags or bins. Have a meeting place in case you get separated from loved ones. If you are on a property, a small boat can come in handy; always have a good rope for towing, rescues, or for tying off. When looking for a place to camp or homestead, find a level area at the top of a small hill or knoll. Avoid the very bottom of a steep hill, alongside a large creek or river, within ten miles of any ocean, or in a low-lying valley.

If the water is rising slowly, turn off utilities to the house, elevate valuables, sanitize and fill tubs and bottles with clean water, tie down items that may get swept away, and retrieve your exodus pack. If the water starts to rise before you can evacuate, move to a second floor, attic, or rooftop, and don't forget your pack.

Do not drive or walk barefoot through flooded roads because floodwaters are toxic. Protect your hands with rubber gloves. Watch out for electrical lines and snakes. Discard any food or medicine that comes into contact with floodwater. Dump mattresses and upholstered furniture, thoroughly wash all linens in hot water, and wipe down everything, including the walls, with a solution of bleach and water. Use bleach to disinfect wells. Hang in there—the water will go down. Usually.

WILDFIRE

Fire is a major concern during the Tribulation as it is one of the devil's favorite tools and a great source of destruction. Already we are seeing major wildfires burning thousands of acres in many countries of the world. It's interesting that God will use fire to cleanse the earth at the end. Both water and fire are necessary for human survival, yet the very same materials can quickly kill. Creation is amazing, isn't it?

The first angel sounded: And hail and fire followed, mingled with blood, and they were thrown to the earth. And a third of the trees were burned up, and all green grass was burned up (Revelation 8:7).

A fire can start from an electrical short, lightning strike, a heater, unattended candles, cooking mishap, gas explosion, mischief, or even a meteor. Or God (or His two witnesses) can just send it on down. (Hey, it's the Tribulation!) Outdoors, any spark can ignite a wildfire, usually unnoticed until flames are leaping from treetop to housetop, consuming acres in short order. Arson is a growing crime and, in the majority of cases, originated by the evil one(s).

Fire Survival Tips

If the government is still working, you may have the assistance of firefighters or dropped flame retardant; however, this is the time to be self-sufficient. To survive a wildfire, a source of water is vital. Ponds and lakes are natural reservoirs, and barrels or cisterns for collecting rainwater are alternate sources. Landscape your home with fire safety in mind by clearing all flammable vegetation, planting more fire resistant hardwood trees and using gravel or stone paths to make a fire line around the circumference of your property. Make sure a garden hose reaches around the house and that there is a way of escape from upper floors via a ladder.

If a wildfire approaches, turn off utilities, close windows and fireplace screens, soak the house and property with copious amounts of water, and then grab your exodus pack and leave the area. Determine which way the wind is blowing and head in the opposite direction. Avoid dry brush and forest, and keep to riverbeds or low ground. Cover your head with a damp cloth and stay low.

For smaller fires, salt makes a good extinguisher. Remove the source of oxygen, if possible. Rocks and cement can contain a fire and keep you in control. If any part of a person is on fire, immediately stop, drop to the floor, and roll until the fire is snuffed out. When in a public place, be sure to notice all exits.

If you happen to be unfortunate and have a meteor or other space debris land in your vicinity, leave the area. Depending on its size, intense heat and a smoldering fire will take months to cool off.

STORMS

There is the common thunderstorm with booms, rain, and lightning; however, certain weather conditions create storms that can grow into a hurricane (also known as a typhoon or cyclone), blizzard, tornado, *derecho* (land hurricane), or *haboob* (sandstorm). Hailstorms are on the increase, along with the size of the hailstones.

The major weather factor in most of these is wind, and the effect is dependent upon what is getting blown around and the velocity of the wind. In tropical and subtropical regions, hurricane season brings on a series of named storms with downpours and gusts, sometimes so great as to destroy buildings, strip trees, and cause serious flooding. A blizzard can dump so much snow in drifts that you can't leave your house. Blowing sand can pulverize all surfaces, including your skin, and leave granules in every crevice. Storms spawn tornadoes—fast moving, whirling dervishes that destroy everything in their path.

Storm Survival Tips

It's always best to seek sturdy shelter in any storm. If a warning is issued, quickly secure outdoor animals, furniture, etc. and then hunker down in your shelter, using the time to gather your survival supplies. Downstairs, underground, or in the strongest room in your house for a tornado; upstairs, away from openings and where you can keep warm in a blizzard. In colder climates, insulate your utility pipes to keep them from freezing and/or bursting.

If you are trapped in your car during a blizzard, stay put, display a brightly colored cloth, and beware of carbon monoxide poisoning. Every half hour, run the engine (and heater) for fifteen minutes. Do not leave your car. Dress in warm layers and watch for signs of frostbite (tissue damage which occurs mostly to the limbs, nose, and ears, with symptoms being numbness and black discoloration of the skin). In the aftermath of a blizzard, stop and rest every few minutes when shoveling snow, and clear off your roof to avoid cave-ins. Be careful when using candles, heaters, and gas stoves.

Hurricane preparation includes boarding up windows, stowing valuables in waterproof containers, and staying put in a strong, interior room with provisions. If you are on the coast and are told to evacuate, then go. Water and electricity may not work after the storm so have enough fresh water and nonperishable food on hand for at least ten days. If you must be outside, locate a place that is protected from the wind and stay low, unless the water level is rising. Do not be fooled by the eye of the hurricane—when all seems calm as the very center of the storm passes over you. The sky may even turn blue and fair! In a few minutes to an hour, the winds pick up again, this time from the other direction. Stay secure in your shelter until you are sure the storm has moved away. Check on your neighbors. You'll most likely need an axe or saw to clear debris and a tarp to cover open windows or roof.

If a sand or dust storm is on the horizon, close all doors and windows and secure plastic sheeting over them; protect your lungs by covering your nose and mouth with a damp cloth or dust mask.

And, of course, even a common thunderstorm contains deadly lightning. Avoid metal, electrical outlets, tall trees or poles, and bodies of water. If caught outside without shelter, lay in a ditch. Be the shortest object in the vicinity.

HEAT AND DROUGHT

Whether due to climate change, Satan's mischief, or God's wrath, extreme heat can be uncomfortable and even deadly. *Then the fourth angel poured out his bowl on the sun, causing it to scorch everyone with its fire. Everyone was burned by this blast of heat, and they cursed the name of God who sent all of these plagues. They did not repent and give him glory* (Revelation 16:8–9 NLT).

People suffer heat-related illness when their bodies are unable to properly cool themselves and sometimes sweating just isn't enough to do the job. Dry heat and high body temperature can damage vital organs. Humid or muggy conditions make the air thick and harder for the body to use evaporation for cooling. A prolonged drought raises the ground temperature, and the increased demand for water and electricity may prompt resource shortages. Heat waves and droughts also cause crop damage resulting in food shortages. Rationing of water may be a reality.

Heat and Drought Survival Tips

Wear loose-fitting, lightweight clothes, in layers. Drink plenty of fluids. Add a pinch of salt and/or sugar to water. Avoid strenuous exercise. If possible, stay in an air-conditioned room with the window blinds or curtains drawn shut to keep out the hot sunshine. If outdoors, seek shade and a pond or some other body of water. Slow down all activity—animals, too—until the weather breaks. Look out for fires. If in a severe drought, pray for rain.

PESTILENCE

This is the word used in the Bible to describe the spread of diseases that is epidemic and deadly. Interesting that the Merriam-Webster dictionary also defines pestilence as "morally, socially, or politically harmful." A lot of that is going on, too! *Pestilence marches before him; plague follows close behind* (Habakkuk 3:5 NLT).

When viruses, bacteria, and fungi grow, the germs are passed from insects, animals, or person-to-person. People spread many diseases as they travel the globe, through sexual activity, hand-to-mouth, or airborne. Biological terrorism can release pathogens that rapidly spread, causing illness and death.

Pestilence Survival Tips

To avoid catching a deadly disease, there are a few precautions you can take. Be somewhat of a loner and avoid crowds. Abstain from non-monogamous sex. Keep your family together if all seem healthy and quarantine the sick in a separate camp as soon as symptoms appear. Wash your hands often and thoroughly with soap and water. Boil all water that you suspect is contaminated. Cook all food thoroughly.

Be sure to get enough sleep, eat the most nutritious foods that are available, and sit out in the sunshine for short periods to keep a healthy immune system. If you have stocked up on medicines, take what you know will treat the problem. Antibiotics don't work on viruses and germs are increasingly resistant to them but they could save your life if bacteria are growing. If a cold or flu lasts more than ten days or if a wound refuses to heal, take the antibiotic. Chlorine bleach can disinfect your clothing, bed sheets, and surfaces.

If you are in a warm and humid climate, a simple tight netting can protect you from flying insects that carry disease. Rodents and other small mammals can carry rabies, parasites, or viruses, so avoid them, especially if they exhibit symptoms like foaming at the mouth or aggressively erratic behavior. And, as always, prayer is the best protection.

FAMINE

An unfortunate effect of these natural occurrences is famine: not enough food to go around. Flooding, drought, and extreme temperatures destroy crops in the field and without proper grass or hay, animals that we use for food cannot survive. Changes in the seas and oceans decimate the fish population. Pestilence not only affects humans but all living things, including the things we eat. Livestock can be infected with parasites, foot rot, trichomoniasis, botulism, etc. The exploding human population alone contributes to food shortages. Politics can even get in the way of food production and distribution by abandoning local farmers, the nationalization of farms, and prohibiting the transportation of relief supplies due to greed, control issues, or political gain.

Famine Survival Tips

The time to plan for a famine is now. Instead of purchasing frivolous items, stock up on canned meats and soups, staples such as flour, rice, and sugar. God warned Joseph about the famine that was to come upon Egypt so he filled the storehouses with seven years' worth of food. (Hmm, seven years…)

Even with our provisions, we need to remember that God is in the business of rewarding those who trust Him on a day-by-day basis. Jesus taught us to pray, *"Give us this day our daily bread"* (Luke 11:3). The manna provided for the wandering Israelites only lasted one day before it spoiled. God has promised to feed the raven, so how much more will He feed us? If we ask for bread, will He give us a stone? Of course not! Ultimately, He is our provider. *"What man is there among you who, if his son asks for bread, will give him a stone? Or if he asks for a fish, will be give him a serpent? If you then, being evil, know how to give good gifts to your children, how much more will your Father who is in heaven give good things to those who ask Him!"* (Matthew 7:9–11).

It is still possible to find food in the natural world. That's the way it's supposed to work—even though modern man has forgotten with the convenience of supermarkets and restaurants. Forage for berries, nuts, and seeds; catch fish, animals and insects; dig for roots; carefully explore abandoned shops or houses, which may yield a pantry.

The importance of community really hits home when everyone contributes to the whole. Searching for food can be time consuming without the availability of a corner market, so the harvest is greater with more people sharing what they find. Your odds of assembling a decent meal increase with the assistance of others.

WILD BEASTS

The Bible says that during the Tribulation, wild beasts attack men. *And power was given to them over a fourth of the earth, to kill with sword, with hunger, with death, and by the beasts of the earth* (Revelation 6:8). Whether Satan possesses them (as when Jesus sent the demons into a herd of swine) or their DNA is affected by chemical or biological agents, or they, too, feel the insanity of the times, wild animals will turn on their higher-ups. They need to eat, too, and will fight to claim their share of food in a famine. Whether bears, alligators, wolves, lions, snakes, a cloned pterodactyl, mutant, or Sasquatch, wild beasts are formidable opponents. *"That day will not bring light and prosperity but darkness and disaster. In that day you will be like a man who runs from a lion, only to meet a bear. After escaping the bear, he leans his hand against a wall and is bitten by a snake. Yes, the day of the Lord will be a dark and hopeless day, without a ray of joy or hope"* (Amos 5:18b–19 NLT).

Wild Beast Survival Tips

Always leave an out—whether to escape from an attacking beast or space for it to make a retreat. Stay clear of dead carcasses, which attract hungry scavengers, and always keep your own food wrapped, covered, and elevated out of reach. Don't attempt to capture a wild animal unless you have the training, protective clothing, restraint equipment, and caging necessary to perform the job. Of course, this is when a shotgun comes in handy. And finally, take hold of your God-given authority of dominion over the animals and command it, in Jesus' name and with faith, to depart.

A Few Words About Your Own Animals

All domestic animals should have some form of identification, such as a tattoo or metal tag securely fastened to a collar or braided in hair. Keep a photo or documents for proof of ownership. Soon the lion will lie down with the lamb, but in the meantime, protect your animals from the wild beasts mentioned above by keeping them within sturdy fencing and providing shelter, food, and water at all times. And don't forget, pets and domestic animals look to us for love, comfort, and direction.

SUPERNATURAL PHENOMENA

There is the natural world that we know, and then there is the supernatural—something that happens outside of our perception of reality and, therefore, somewhat of a mystery, making it difficult to explain or predict.

With Satan and his demons running around loose and men searching for power in all the wrong places, supernatural activity is at an all-time high. It seems that when times are confusing, people look for answers beyond themselves. Instead of turning to God or the Bible for answers, they consult psychics, mediums, tarot cards, Oujia boards, crystals, aliens, and false religions. UFOs are supernatural in origin—aliens are not from other planets but rather demons in disguise to deceive and distract mankind. The Antichrist and his false prophet utilize supernatural power to attain their total domination and enslavement through an easily deceived population.

The Nephilim were a race of giants conceived by demons having sex with humans. Since that was one of the reasons God destroyed the world with the Flood, and the Bible says that the end times would be like in the times of Noah, these powerful, semi-supernatural beings may make a comeback during the Tribulation.

God, too, uses supernatural power to get mankind's attention and to dole out judgment. *Then locusts came from the smoke and descended on the earth and they were given power to sting like scorpions. They were told ... to attack all the people who did not have the seal of God on their foreheads. They were told not to kill them but to torture them for five months with agony like the pain of scorpion stings. In those days people will seek death but will not find it* (Revelation 9:3–6 NLT).

Supernatural Phenomena Survival Tips

This is when you'd better be on your knees and asking God for mercy and protection. Avoid any indication of occult activity. In fact, run the other way!

Be sure of what you believe and don't waver; resist the devil and he will flee from you. Speak Scripture as the Sword of Truth and put on the whole armor of God to defend yourself from the evil one. Stand firm in humility but pray in the power and authority of Jesus' name.

ENVIRONMENTALISM

One of mankind's directives from God was to tend the earth. *God blessed them [Adam and Eve] and told them, "Multiply and fill the earth and subdue it. Be masters over the fish and birds and all the animals"* (Genesis 1:28 NLT). It is obvious from the condition of today's earth that we have failed miserably in this task. However, much of the problem is due to sin and thus, the curse.

Some may think that this subject should be under Man-made Catastrophes. Global warming activists believe that it's humanity's fault. Earth Day has become a worldwide holy day. Anyone caught wasting energy or creating too much trash is publicly humiliated or fined. I was filling up my car at a gas station while cleaning out my car of some empty water bottles. As I threw them in the trash, I was reprimanded by a lady at the next pump for not recycling them (which I do when I can). It seems that being "green" is paramount to any other cause.

But if you've read this far, you know that it's too late for stopgap measures; our planet is too far-gone to fix the damage. Because Satan holds the deed to the earth at this time, we can't expect everything to be all clean and beautiful! *For we know that the whole creation groans and labors with birth pangs together until now* (Romans 8:22). All of nature is groaning for redemption, and the earth has become the grand prize in an ages-old spiritual battle.

Environmentalism Survival Tips

Although it's too late to reverse environmental damage, it makes sense to conserve resources, to protect existing wild areas, to plant trees, to recycle, to not pollute or litter, and to be ecologically minded. Treat animals well, but remember that they are not more important than humans. Mother Earth is not an entity but a nickname for the creation of an almighty God. Whatever small patch of the earth or creature is in your care, obey God's command to tend His garden.

UNUSUAL NATURAL DISASTERS

During the Tribulation, many events will be unprecedented making it difficult to advise you on survival tactics, such as:

- One-third of the earth, one-third of the trees, and all the green grass will be destroyed from hail and fire. (Revelation 8:7)

- One-third of the sea becomes blood and one-third of all living things in the sea die due to a meteor or comet [a mountain of fire thrown into the sea]. (Revelation 8:8–9)
- A star called Wormwood falls out of the sky and makes all of the water bitter and many people die. (Revelation 8:10–11)
- Darkness fills the land as one-third of the sun is struck and one-third of the moon, and one-third of the stars become dark. (Revelation 8:12)

Never forget that God is still on His throne, and the best survival tip of all is to stay close to Him. If you are His friend, everything will be okay.

Chapter 12
MAN-MADE CATASTROPHES

Our scientific power has outrun our spiritual power.
We have guided missiles and misguided men.

MARTIN LUTHER KING, JR.

A s if it's not enough having to deal with the wrath of God and dodging the devil, the depravity of mankind causes more catastrophes. War and violence, revolution and rebellion, nuclear and biological weapons, pollution and consumption, clones and robots, super-inflation and economic collapse, surveillance and totalitarianism. As the heart of man increasingly grows cold and everyone struggles to survive, anarchy and chaos prevail. Mayhem ensues, at least until the Antichrist takes severe measures to bring all into compliance.

You should also know this…that in the last days there will be very difficult times. For people will love only themselves and their money. They will be boastful and proud, scoffing at God, disobedient to their parents and ungrateful. They will consider nothing sacred. They will be unloving and unforgiving, they will slander others and have no self-control; they will be cruel and have no interest in what is good. They will betray their friends, be reckless, be puffed up with pride, and love pleasure rather than God (2 Timothy 3:1–4 NLT).

VIOLENCE AND WAR

Ever since Cain killed Abel, the inclination to hurt another person, sometimes to the death, has grown like a cancer. The news is full of armed robberies, rapes, domestic abuse, murders, hate crimes, slavery, road rage, torture, homeless beatings, elderly muggings, piracy, kidnappings, drive-by shootings, gang fights, terrorism. Something called the knock-out game is the latest trend—young thugs hitting people from behind on their heads until they fall down. Many of those attacked are the elderly—those who used to be respected!

People even harm themselves with cutting, tattoos, extreme sports, unusual body piercings, drug abuse, embedding objects under the skin (devil horns!), excessive cosmetic surgery, and suicide. Cruelty depicted in movies and on television has made us numb to its consequences, and violent video games have stolen the innocence of our youth.

Terrorism is a man-made problem that is quite unpredictable because the attacks are stealthily planned and executed. Often there is no warning and an attack can be chemical, biological or physical, or a combination. Terrorists attempt to conquer through fear, causing people to be afraid to travel or even go shopping. The day the World Trade Center fell—buildings that I had been atop—made me realize that an enemy can be brutal and deranged and that anything can happen. Even on a clear, sky-blue Tuesday morning.

War is the ultimate act of violence and in abundance during this dread time as nations, regions, factions, and neighbors fight about everything from perceived slights to the boundaries of the Holy Land.

When the Restrainer—or, the Holy Spirit—leaves the earth at the Rapture, evil and sin increase exponentially. The world is devoid of love and full of hate. Wickedness reaches new levels only imagined in nightmares and horror films—a human being can become devilish in nature. It takes a special mercy from God to endure and to keep your light shining brightly.

Violence Survival Tips

As always, the first line of defense is to put on the whole armor of God. Depending on the situation, it may be time to hide, flee, or fight.

Hiding is easiest in a rural, forested area. The tree canopy blocks the view from aircraft and satellites; however, heat seeking or scanning technology can still detect you. Land formations in mountainous regions may make it easier to keep out of sight and caves can be great hiding places. Use camouflage and, if necessary, play dead. Keep a low profile wherever you are by not drawing attention to yourself. Live a simple life, dress modestly, and avoid trouble. And though it's best to stay away from large populations (with its greater chance for confrontations, surveillance, tattling, and terrorism), there can be safety in numbers. Getting together with a group of like-minded people provides support, comfort, and security.

Sometimes it is necessary to flee. Grab your exodus pack, plus whatever else you can bring, and retreat to a less-populated area. Note all possible routes to and from your location and identify the exits out of public buildings. The quickly changing geopolitical landscape makes it hard to determine where the safest locations may be at this time, but again, a rural area can buy you time. It's important to be aware of your surroundings at all times, including any strangers.

Be sensitive to the guidance from God's still, small voice. He has already warned Israel that when the abomination of desolation occurs in the middle of the Tribulation, the Jews should flee into the wilderness (possibly Petra in Jordan). *She [Israel] was given two wings like those of a great eagle. This allowed her to fly to a place prepared for her in the wilderness, where she would be cared for and protected from the dragon for a time, times and half a time* [3¹/₂ years] (Revelation 12:14 NLT).

And sometimes, you may need to fight. Learn some basic self-defense moves, such as stepping on your opponent's instep, kneeing the groin area, poking the eyes. Use any available weapon if you must, and even a cast-iron frying pan or baseball bat can stop your assailant cold. A gun may prove to be a good friend.

When facing down evil, *Resist the devil and he will flee from you* (James 4:7). Use memorized Scripture as your weapon. Heed the words of the Two Witnesses or the 144,000 Jews. Though they may preach only of salvation, in a world where many voices are calling out to you, they speak the Voice of Truth.

If you are burning with righteous indignation, you may decide to go to war. Soldiering in this time is not for the faint of heart, but, if you are fighting for freedom and truth, it is a noble and courageous mission. Remember that death is not the worst thing that can happen. However, if you choose to join the Antichrist's army, you're the walking dead.

Since 9/11, airline passengers are understandably jumpy. To increase the likelihood of survival during a hijacking, remember that the hijackers were subject to the same screening process as you, so (1) form a team; (2) gather items that can be used as weapons; and (3) create a diversion. Then roll!

In the event of an explosion in a train, plane, or building, get out as fast as you safely can. If trapped, get down on the floor under a heavy piece of furniture and cover your face. Perhaps you have a working cell phone or can use the whistle from your exodus pack to summon help. Learn CPR and first aid to assist loved ones that may get injured in a confrontation.

NUCLEAR ATTACKS

Ever since the first use of an atomic bomb in the 1940s, the world has been fearful of any nation detonating this catastrophic weapon of mass destruction. As the technology has evolved, fusion or H-bombs have replaced fission or atomic bombs. A nuclear bomb can be exploded in the atmosphere over a country in an EMP (electromagnetic pulse), rendering all electricity and electronics useless, maybe for more than a year. An EMP attack would shut down power grids, computers, cars, and communication devices. Radiation may be minimal but the disruption to daily life would be enormous.

A neutron bomb leaves buildings standing while destroying just people and animals—a description eerily similar to Zechariah 14:12: *Their flesh shall dissolve while they stand on their feet, their eyes shall dissolve in their sockets, and their tongues shall dissolve in their mouths.* Nuclear power plants are useful for providing clean energy but accidents do happen in which radiation is released. Irradiating food destroys pests; however, many consumers have a fear of being poisoned by the very food that we need to live.

Radioactive materials are composed of atoms that are unstable, which give off energy until they become stable. The energy emitted is radiation. People naturally receive radiation through the sun, elements in the soil and rocks, and also from household appliances and medical x-rays. The longer a person is exposed to radiation and the closer a person is to the source determines the risk. Too much radiation is deadly to the body. It cannot be detected by our senses but is evaluated through Geiger counters or other gauging instruments. During the "walking ghost phase" of radiation poisoning, a person may feel okay but will die in short order.

Radiation Survival Tips

Usually an emergency event of this severity is announced through warning sirens in the streets or signals on radio, television, and the Internet. If you are within a mile of ground zero, you will die. If you are a few miles out, you'll have ten to fifteen seconds until the heat wave hits you and maybe twenty to thirty minutes until the shock wave does. Do not look at the flash! The hot wind peaks at about 600 mph and will level anything or anybody. The blast zone radiates for about twenty miles from the center.

Many people will be affected by radiation fallout, which is the dust and debris that becomes toxic. This fallout may rain down as contaminated black soot, known as black rain. Before fallout arrives, you might try to cover up items outside that you want to protect, such as feed and hay, firewood, garden plots, and rain barrels. Close and lock all windows and doors; turn off air conditioning and generally seal up any openings. Bring pets inside and provide as much shelter as possible for livestock. Crops already harvested should be brought inside. Thoroughly wash and peel any fruits or vegetables that may have become contaminated. Be sure you've stocked up on food and water to last several weeks.

If you are in, or can get to, a sturdy shelter with thick walls, go to the center of the building. Anything you can shore the walls up with will help. Four inches of concrete, six inches of brick or gravel, seven inches of earth, ten inches of water, or eighteen inches of wood can provide a barrier from harmful fallout.[1] Plan on staying in your shelter for a minimum of two hundred hours (eight to nine days). Cars are not adequate shelter. The authorities will let you know when it's safe to go outside.

Keep covered with clothing (hats, gloves, closed long sleeves and pants, goggles) especially when outside. If you come in from outside, remove outer clothing, including shoes, and discard outside in a sealed plastic bag. Wash your skin with soap and water. Do not use hair conditioner, as it will bind radioactive material to your hair.

Exposure to fallout doesn't make you radioactive, but you need to minimize inhaling it with the help of respirators or dust masks. According to the FDA, keep a supply of potassium iodide (KI) tablets.[2] Depending on body weight and age, one 130 mg. tablet would help if taken soon after the attack. If unavailable, apply a tablespoon of Betadine or iodine tincture to the abdomen. (Never drink iodine.) Do not take acetaminophen in a radioactive emergency because it depletes glutathione and slows the body's ability to make new blood. Brazil nuts, blackstrap molasses, and whey protein isolate boosts glutathione.

Animals are sensitive to radiation damage, too, and need the same protections as humans to survive. Livestock housed in barns during fallout have a better chance of surviving than those outside. Make sure their feed and water is protected inside too.

Remember, in a nuclear emergency, you need to limit the amount of radiation that you are exposed to. Think about shielding, distance, and time.

- Shielding: You will be exposed to less radiation if you have a thick shield between yourself and the radioactive fallout. Walls do not need to be made of lead, as you can be adequately protected behind thick walls of concrete or even wood.
- Distance: The further away you are from the blast and fallout, the lower your exposure. Generally, you are safe if you are more than fifty miles away.
- Time: Minimizing your time exposed to radiation reduces your risk, and the threat diminishes over time as the radioactive material decays.

CHEMICAL AND BIOLOGICAL ATTACKS

A chemical attack is the deliberate release of a toxic gas, liquid, or solid that poisons people and the environment. A biological attack is the deliberate release of germs or other biological substances that make you sick. Some cause contagious illnesses that spread through the population; others like anthrax are not contagious but a very small amount is deadly.

Released into the air in a populous area or added to the water supply, these type of attacks are difficult to contain and can be most catastrophic. A release of deadly agents does not necessarily lead to exposure because you must come into contact with it through the skin, the lungs, or ingestion.

Most of the chemical or biological agents used to kill are odorless or tasteless, and thus are difficult to detect.

Chemical and Biological Attack Survival Tips

If your eyes are watering, your skin is stinging, or you're having trouble breathing, you may have been exposed to a chemical. Be alert to the possible presence of an agent, such as an oily film on surfaces, dead or dying birds in the area, unexplained odors, low clouds of suspended materials, colored vapor, or people wearing protective masks.

If you suspect an attack, leave the area immediately and get to fresh air. Go to the highest ground possible as most chemical elements are heavier than air and will sink to low-lying areas. Remove your clothing without letting it touch your face, and wash thoroughly with soap and water, being careful not to rub the agent into your skin. Rinse your eyes with copious amounts of clear water. If you have ingested a caustic chemical, do not induce vomiting as it may cause further damage to your esophagus on its way back up. A universal poison antidote consists of 2 parts activated charcoal, 1 part strong tea, and 1 part milk of magnesia.[3]

If you are indoors when a chemical agent is released, stay there. Seal the windows and doors and wait for an all-clear announcement.

A biological attack may take a few days to manifest. Public health officials may not be able to provide immediate information about what exactly has been released. If you become aware of any unusual or suspicious release of toxins, protect yourself by moving away from the affected area. Cover your mouth and nose with fabric and avoid spreading germs by washing your hands with soap and water regularly. A plain chlorine bleach solution (10:1) kills many germs and should be used as the emergency passes. Talcum powder absorbs harmful agents on the skin if water isn't available.

Unfortunately, the symptoms of most biological attacks need the use of certain medicines and professional medical attention.

POLLUTION

When God created the earth, it was as a self-sustaining organism. Animals and plants would reproduce after their own kind. Water would evaporate into the air where it would gather in clouds and fall down as rain to start the cycle all over again, as a way of controlling temperature, growing crops, cleansing the air, and being readily available for the myriad uses we humans use water for. The Cycle of Life where nothing is wasted. Even corpses are utilized by bugs, which decompose and are absorbed into dirt.

Whether as a result of sin or man's consumption of stuff, the earth has been polluted in almost every locale. Factories belch toxic clouds into the air, chemicals into the ground, and wastewater into rivers and lakes. Even farms can harm the soil with fertilizer and refuse. Cruise ships dump garbage overboard, and oil spills kill wildlife and irritate skin. There's even the Great Pacific Garbage Patch that stretches for hundreds of miles across the northern Pacific Ocean, a vortex forming a floating junkyard. The west coast of the United States is getting inundated with debris years after the Japanese earthquake and accompanying tsunami. Sloppy, disrespectful people litter our cities and suburban byways with trash. Millions of motor vehicles spew exhaust fumes causing smog that blocks the sun and fills our lungs. Our resources have been contaminated.

There's also noise pollution from roadways, industries, and sirens. There is hardly anywhere left where the sound of an airplane flying overhead isn't heard. Illumination in our towns and cities, as well as artificial light from satellites and airplanes, cause light pollution, which deny us a glimpse of the starry sky. Visual blight is growing, destroying the view with power lines, billboards, trash dumps, graffiti, poles, and litter.

Pristine areas are getting harder to find, and it is practically impossible to completely avoid pollution in this fallen world.

Pollution Survival Tips

It's been said, "The solution to pollution is dilution." In the past when technologies were simpler and byproducts more benign, flooding the pollutant with water worked well. Nowadays the irritants are more complex and much more difficult to disperse. Fleeing the polluted area may not be an option.

Any barrier of protection is preferable to nakedness. Clothing and gloves protect skin; dust masks or bandannas filter air particles. Do not swim or drink from polluted waters. If there is smog so thick you can see it, stay indoors with the windows closed or move to a higher elevation above the dirty air.

Efforts to save the planet from global warming or pollution are admirable, but it's too late. The damage is done; nature is wearing out. Enforcing more regulations that limit production will negatively affect the economy and quality of life. But ultimately, humans are not in control of Earth, as Satan holds sway until Jesus returns. Our planet will not get clean and pure until God cleanses and purifies it with fire. Meanwhile, try to avoid the more polluted areas and do not contribute to the problem. Keep your little section of the world clean.

ARTIFICIAL LIFE FORMS

The ultimate sin of humanistic pride is to imitate the Creator by making artificial beings in the "image of man." Mankind wants to control its own race and the environment, and scientists are only too happy to accommodate. Cloning began with a sheep named Dolly, and it's not clear how far it will go. The movie, *Jurassic Park*, showed what happens when dinosaurs are re-created. Imagine someone uses your grandparents' DNA to "resurrect" them again by growing them from a Petri dish. This opens up a whole Pandora's box of issues about morality and reality. Does anyone know if a clone possesses a spirit, or soul? Is it okay to enslave them?

Or is that what robots are for? To create an artificial being that is at our beck and call—to be servants or actually slaves, since they won't be getting paid for their work. Science fiction movies have been full of robots, both cute and menacing, from *Star Wars* to *I, Robot*. We've been warned about the dangers of robots and machines since the 1950s. Can they become so self-aware that they rebel? Would they kill a human? Can demons possess them and bring them to life?

Although various machines have proved to be amazing and helpful creations of man, a fully functioning robot would be the ultimate product. A Japanese man has put together a fem-bot (a robot that substitutes for a girlfriend)—a Stepford wife without the mess of a red-blooded woman. According to Human Rights Watch, fully autonomous weapons, known as "killer robots," would be able to select and engage targets without human intervention. This can be a nightmare scenario because it would be hard to stop an entire army of killer robots.

We actually create the very monsters that can harm us, physically and emotionally. Virtual reality creates artificial scenarios through manipulation of the brain. A cyborg is a person who is dependent upon computer processes or implants to function. Scientists are trying to meld insect DNA and nano machinery to create miniature drones.

Holograms are three-dimensional images of a person or object that can communicate in real time and may be the image of the Antichrist that the False Prophet forces the population to worship.

Artificial Life Survival Tips

Since they're not mentioned in the Bible, I don't believe that clones or robots will have the time or wherewithal to become a major catastrophe. The devil cannot hand out souls, but he is skilled at causing trouble, so don't be a party to human cloning or artificial creation. Cloning of a person's own internal organs or appendages is a medical marvel and having a robot perform certain functions is an amazing tool, but we cannot allow people to create these monsters. However, I believe that Jesus shows up before matters get out of hand—before mankind can complete its prideful and unnatural creations. I hope I'm right.

And because it's the most important thing not to do during the Tribulation, I will repeat it again: do not worship the image of the Antichrist!

COMPUTERS, SURVEILLANCE, AND TOTALITARIANISM

The first computers were so large that they filled a whole room, but now they fit in the palm of a hand—even *in* your hand. The computer in my car is smarter and more sophisticated than the computers that were onboard the spacecraft that first brought astronauts to the moon! They have become the tools of most trades. This book was written and published with the aid of computers. They assist in manufacturing, engineering, space missions, mathematics, medicine, finance, retail, music, and the arts. Supermarket checkouts are computers, and actors can be computer animated.

The computer spawned the Internet, which has become the town square, corner market, newspaper, dating service, classroom, and village hussy. Kids spend hours playing interactive video games with people across the world. Voyeurs and exhibitionists have found a new outlet. The cashless society is already functioning on the Internet with online billing and e-commerce. Cyber attacks can cripple the financial and transportation sectors.

Like most objects, a computer can be used for good or evil. It has the potential to be used for great evil. The Bible says that the Antichrist initiates a worldwide system of total control, which is only possible with the information-gathering ability of a computer and the location-finding ability of a GPS.

Even now, it is possible to plot the whereabouts of a person by their cell phone or know when they drove on a certain highway using an electronic transponder affixed to their car. Every product and package is given an RFID chip (a giant step up from the static bar code). Radio frequency identification chips can be read from a distance to track information and delivery status. I need to wave a badge to get into my office, which is recorded in the security department with my photo and time of entry and exit. In the interest of homeland security, backscatter scanners examine vehicles and buildings without a search warrant, while airplane passengers are scanned or patted down in an invasion of privacy. The surveillance society is here with cameras in all public spaces, satellites with a magnified birds-eye view of our backyards, and tiny drones that peer in your windows. Our privacy is gone as almost every street in the world has been mapped and filmed by Google Earth and posted online for all to see.

Animals are injected with microchips in case they get lost, and it won't be long before prisoners, immigrants, and old people get chipped so they can be found if they escape or wander away. That day may already be here by the time you read this! With increased robbery and identity thefts, the smartest solution, so it seems, is to just microchip or barcode everyone. No more lost or stolen credit cards, identity theft, medical info readily available in case of emergency, finding anyone you deem missing. Sounds like a great idea. However, the Antichrist uses this technology to know and record everything about everyone, and ultimately to control everyone, that is, everyone who takes the mark of the beast.

The Antichrist will be the most heinous dictator the world has ever seen. That's a pretty strong distinction considering history has already suffered through Nero, Hitler, Stalin, Mao, and Mussolini. Socialism, communism, and Nazism are slippery slopes to a totalitarian society—when the government leaders think they know what's best for the people. They want to control the economy, media, morality, education, transportation, employment, private property, and the weather if they could. The Antichrist even wants to change the time. He certainly couldn't have the calendar read AD—Anno Domini—in the Year of Our Lord. *He shall speak pompous words against the Most High, shall persecute the saints of the Most High, and shall intend to change times and law* (Daniel 7:25).

Dictators are fond of a science called *eugenics*, which aims to improve future generations by eliminating "inferior" humans. Of course this goes against the fact that every human is created in the image of God with intrinsic value. To reach their goal of a perfect society, various methods are used: infanticide, selective breeding, genetic counseling, genome mapping, abortion, forced sterilization, euthanasia, and genocide. The Nazis were notorious for performing experimental atrocities on prisoners to reach the limits of torture. Power to shape the world to his liking brings about the ultimate horrors of the New World Order under the Antichrist.

Computers, Surveillance, and Totalitarianism Survival Tips

Computers are such a part of our world that it's almost impossible to get through the day without one. It isn't necessary to throw yours out the window if you are cautious. To avoid identity theft and being party to the cashless society, don't purchase items online. Support your local businesses and meet your neighborhood storeowners. Refrain from paying your bills online if writing checks is still an option. However, this practice is already getting frowned upon as businesses dangle discounts for switching to electronic payments. They say it's to save the trees, but it's really about them saving money. Before you trash a computer, erase your files and zero out the hard drive.

Do not give out your Social Security Number or other National (or Global?) Identification Number to just anyone who asks. Confirm that it is on a need-to-know basis and to those who are officially authorized to have that information. Keep a low profile, electronically speaking. Make sure you can throw your cell phone away, disconnect your personal computer, deactivate social networking accounts, or disengage your global positioning system. Just cut the darn thing out of your car or wherever it may be—even under your skin!

During the Tribulation, it is best to live a simple life. Learn to function without electricity or electronics. You cannot expect privacy and security so blend in and keep a low profile. Obey the authorities until they cross the laws of God, which always takes precedence. Stay quiet but not silent. Stand up for what you believe, even if you face death. Patrick Henry said, "Give me liberty or give me death."

SUPER-INFLATION

Saving for that proverbial rainy day may be good advice, but is no guarantee that it will protect you in a time of super-inflation, which the Bible foretells is an economic reality during the Tribulation.

One of the major causes of the stock market crash of 1929 was due to investors buying stock on margin when they didn't actually have the cash available. Soon the amount of loans was more than the amount of currency circulating. As I write this, nations around the world are printing paper money that isn't backed by anything of worth. The cause of super-inflation—or hyperinflation—is a rapid and massive increase in the amount of money that is not supported by corresponding growth of goods and services, which results in an imbalance between the supply and demand for the money. Whenever a nation has too much debt, their currency becomes devalued. Prices of necessary goods rise dramatically while salaries diminish. *And a voice from among the four living beings said, "A loaf of wheat bread or three loaves of barley for a day's pay. And don't waste the olive oil and wine"* (Revelation 6:6 NLT).

Super-inflation Survival Tips

The Tribulation is not the time to splurge on luxurious or unnecessary items. Trading paper money for gold or silver won't protect you. You can't eat gold! *"They will throw their silver into the streets, and their gold will be like refuse; their silver and their gold will not be able to deliver them in the day of the wrath of the LORD"* (Ezekiel 7:19). Make a budget and stick to it. When you find necessities at a good price, get extra. And as discussed previously, bartering may be the answer to your inflation situation.

AMUSEMENTS

I'm sure the title of this portion is unexpected, but people have invented myriad ways and devices to amuse, which can destroy the soul. The word "muse" means "to think" and the prefix "a" means "not" so "to amuse" means "to not think." All of the things that we use to amuse ourselves are basically tools of the devil to keep us from thinking hard about the important matters in life—about our behavior, about life and death, about God. Any thing that keeps people from thinking about their eternal destiny or their need for God's salvation is catastrophic to that person.

Man pursues amusements to dull the pain of his hopeless and miserable life and we willingly give in to the devil's temptations to keep us busy with television, the Internet, sports, movies, alcohol, smart phones, illicit sex, drugs, video games, shopping, roller coasters, parties, theme parks, concerts, excessive exercise, casinos, the foibles of the rich and famous, gourmet food, toys—the list is practically endless.

It is difficult to spend Sunday morning in church when the football game is beckoning. Instead of quiet time to reflect, we leave the television on for background noise and blast music from our car radios. Teenagers can't go anywhere without buds in their ears and little old ladies find strange comfort in the whizzing and buzzing of slot machines or the excitement of bingo halls. We "tweet" our every move and spend hours on networking sites and cell phones spilling our guts to whoever will listen, while face-to-face family time and our prayer life suffers.

Amusement Survival Tips

"Be still and know that I am God" (Psalm 46:10). Turn off the television, step away from the computer, say good-bye, and hang up the phone. There's too much talking going on and not enough contemplation. Again, the amusement itself is not evil, but don't allow it to distract you from the real meaning of life and to divert you from spending quality time with your family and friends. Pay attention to your dinner mates instead of your smart phone. Limit how much time you spend being entertained. Stay out of amusement parks!

Everyone needs a sanctuary—a place of privacy and peace where you can be alone and spend time with God. It can be as small as a closet or as lavish as a secret garden, and maybe the only place available is in your own mind.

Take three deep breaths: inhale deeply through your nose, hold for four seconds, and exhale gently through your mouth. Close your eyes or gaze at nature while you talk to God. Get on your knees if it aids your concentration and humility. Prayer should consist of four parts: thanksgiving, repentance, adoration, and supplication, which is making your requests known to God. Then sit quietly for ten or fifteen minutes, waiting for that still, small voice to offer you guidance and comfort. You will feel refreshed and peaceful, knowing that you've spent your time wisely. Your only obsession should be Jesus.

Chapter 13
A MIGHTY FORTRESS

Never be afraid to trust an unknown future to a known God.

CORRIE TEN BOOM

During the Tribulation, people's hearts fail them from the fear of what is happening in the world. Some shake their fists at God with blame and rebellion, refusing to repent and accept His offer of salvation. Many wonder what exactly is truth in a world full of deception. Most take the mark of the beast in fear of persecution and to provide for their families.

However, for those who make the difficult—yet so very easy—decision to accept God's offer, He is a strong foundation, an immovable rock in the storms of life. For God is the same yesterday, today, and tomorrow. He does not change and is faithful to fulfill His promises. His plan goes forward until it reaches fruition. We are privy to these plans so we can know how it all ends—that the victory belongs to Jesus, which gives us incredible hope, confidence, and perseverance. *Bow down your ear to me, deliver me speedily, be my rock of refuge, a fortress of defense to save me* (Psalm 31:2).

THE SOLID TRUTH

In the midst of a profusion of lies and deceit, it is necessary to pay close attention to the Voice of Truth. *All your words are true; all your righteous laws are eternal* (Psalm 119:160 NLT).

Truth can be found in the Bible. Hopefully, you have a copy of your own during the Tribulation. But if not, even amidst all of the evil, I do believe that you will be able to find one somewhere, so try to get your hands on one. Search the homes of raptured saints, in old churches, thrift stores, or libraries. *The words of the Lord are pure words, like silver tried in a furnace of earth, purified seven times. You shall keep them, O LORD, You shall preserve them from this generation forever* (Psalm 12:6–7).

Of course, if you're having trouble obtaining a Bible, there are many Scriptures in this book and others that may have gone under the radar. Read them every chance you get to build your faith and shore up your courage. Memorize key verses that refute the heresies of the day so you can remind yourself what is true, ignoring all other distortions and distractions. *For everything that was written in the past was written to teach us, so that through endurance and the encouragement of the Scriptures we might have hope* (Romans 15:4 NLT).

The Truth is also found in the words of the Two Witnesses who proclaim God's message in Jerusalem and broadcast throughout the earth. *"And I will give power to my two witnesses, and they will be clothed in sackcloth and will prophesy during those 1,260 days* [3¹/₂ years]*"* (Revelation 11:3).

FELLOWSHIP

Meet regularly with other believers, most likely in secret (underground), and share prayer requests, communion, praise reports, necessities, and sound doctrine. They say that misery loves company, and it will comfort you knowing that you're not the only person left in the world who believes in Jesus Christ. Imagine how wonderful it will be in the New Heaven and on the New Earth. Those happy thoughts have enabled believers to "keep on keepin' on" for centuries, and they will help you, too. *Let us not give up meeting together, as some are in the habit of doing, but let us encourage one another—and all the more as you see the Day approaching* (Hebrews 10:25).

Since church buildings have probably been turned into enlightenment centers, museums, or mosques—and you risk persecution if you exhibit a cross—it may be hard to find fellow Christians. The early believers had a system of identifying one another. They would draw a curved line in the dirt or sand, and if the other person completed the picture by drawing the bottom curved line to create the picture of a fish, he or she was a Christian. Of course, this isn't much of a secret sign anymore. Love is the greatest indicator. *"By this all will know that you are My disciples, if you have love for one another"* (John 13:35).

PRAYER

If you happen to be by yourself or lacking any direction, remember you're never totally alone. Keep the line of communication open between you and God at all times with prayer. Ask Him for guidance and discernment. His still, small voice will answer you. He will give you the strength you need to survive, a way out, or the courage to lay down your life. Learn to run to God. When you surrender your will, then He does His best work. Remember that He loves you and cares about you. *For the eyes of the LORD are on the righteous, and His ears are open to their prayers* (1 Peter 3:12a; Psalm 34:17).

Ecclesiastes (and a golden oldie) tells us that there is a time and a season for everything. Now may not be the time to be happy but don't worry. I've presented some fearful scenarios in this book; however, everything is going to turn out great! Worrying proves that you aren't trusting God. We are admonished not to worry about anything but to pray about everything.

It is time to trust the Lord with everything that you have. If you shift your faith in the government, your bank account, or your good deeds to the Lord instead, you will lessen your anxiety because you'll be putting your faith in the One who has promised to look after you and who is mighty to save. 1 Thessalonians 5:17 says to *"pray without ceasing."* Pray for loved ones; pray for Israel; pray for God's kingdom to come on earth as it is in heaven. Keep a prayer on your lips and His Word in your heart at all times. The joy of the Lord and what is to come are your strengths. Keep your eyes on the prize. You can do this!

REVIVAL

In looking at the morass of evil and general disregard for the things of God all around me, it seems it would take a miracle for another great revival to occur. The last revival was in the early 1970s with the Jesus Movement—when I got saved. The Bible says that the Tribulation will not come *unless the falling away comes first* (2 Thessalonians 2:3). I had mentioned previously that this "falling away" could mean a departure from the faith or the departure known as the Rapture, or both. Revival starts with you and me. How many Christians are on their knees and fasting for a revival? Not enough.

It seems that we are living in a post-Christian society where the majority of people have turned away from "old-fashioned" religion. And while that is true, it is also true that now is a time of great harvest. Jesus said, *"Upon this rock I will build my Church and the gates of hell won't prevail against it"* (Matthew 16:18). Folks are still going forward for salvation at each Sunday service during my church's altar calls. Every day, in every country of the world, more people are coming to Jesus and will continue to do so until His return at the end.

After the Rapture of the Church, maybe the greatest revival of all time will occur during the Tribulation. We sometimes think only of gloom and doom, but multitudes come to faith in Jesus at this time. The Two Witnesses, the 144,000 Jews, and the proclaiming angel preach the gospel to every creature. *And I saw another angel flying through the heavens, carrying the everlasting Good News to preach to the people who belong to this world—to every nation, tribe, language and people* (Revelation 14:6). And while the horrors of the Tribulation cause many to shake their fists at God, they scare others enough to finally accept the hope that salvation offers.

Don't shy away from sharing the fact that hell exists. The Law must be given so that a person sees their own sin, and thus, their great need for a Savior. You cannot sow the seed of the gospel without first hoeing and preparing the ground with blunt instruments. It is the Law that shows us our sin. When the Ten Commandments were removed from public schools, generations of children were left in the dark with no moral absolutes. It takes the passion and repentance that comes with understanding our sin to create revival.

Only the Church has been promised the gift of eternal security with the indwelt Holy Spirit as our down payment. It's important to understand that the game changes during the Tribulation after the Age of Grace has ended and, unfortunately, salvation is now dependent on obedience, as well as faith in Jesus' sacrifice—and most likely death as the ultimate test of faith.

Nevertheless, a great revival will save many. *These are the ones who come out of the Great Tribulation, and washed their robes and made them white in the blood of the Lamb. Therefore they are before the throne of God, and serve*

Him day and night in His temple. And He who sits on the throne will dwell among them. They shall neither hunger anymore nor thirst anymore; the sun shall not strike them, or any heat; for the Lamb who is in the midst of the throne will shepherd them and lead them to living fountains of waters. And God will wipe away every tear from their eyes (Revelation 7:14–17).

These are the martyrs who get saved during the Tribulation and die because of their faith. God gives them back everything they lost. They were scorched in the sun and endured pain and suffering but now God reverses their trials into joy. (This verse also shows us that it will be unbearably hot—global warming to the max!)

A great spiritual awakening will occur in all of Israel. The Jewish people come to faith because Jesus will not return to Israel until they welcome Him as their Messiah. *"For I say to you, you shall see me no more till you say 'Blessed is He who comes in the name of the LORD'"* (Matthew 23:39).

THE PROMISES OF GOD

God's promises say it better than I ever could. We have the assurance that God is working in the world on our behalf. The following are some to memorize:

"Therefore I say to you, do not worry about your life, what you will eat or what you will drink; nor about your body, what you will put on. Is not life more than food and the body more than clothing? Look at the birds of the air, for they neither sow nor reap nor gather into barns; yet your heavenly Father feeds them. Are you not of more value than they? Which of you by worrying can add one cubit to his stature? So why do you worry about clothing? Consider the lilies of the field, how they grow: they neither toil nor spin, and yet I say to you that even Solomon in all his glory was not arrayed like one of these. Now if God so clothes the grass of the field, which today is and tomorrow is thrown into the oven, will He not much more clothe you, O you of little faith?"

MATTHEW 6:25–30

But those who wait on the LORD shall renew their strength; they shall mount up with wings like eagles; they shall run and not be weary; they shall walk and not faint.

ISAIAH 40:31

The Lord is my rock and my fortress and my deliverer.

2 SAMUEL 22:2

God's truth stands firm like a foundation stone.

2 TIMOTHY 2:19 NLT

"In the world you will have tribulation, but be of good cheer, I have overcome the world!"

JOHN 16:33b

"For I know the plans I have for you," says the LORD. "They are plans for good and not for disaster, to give you a future and a hope."

JEREMIAH 29:11 NLT

"They shall neither hunger anymore nor thirst anymore; the sun shall not strike them, nor any heat; for the Lamb who is in the midst of the throne will shepherd them and lead them to living fountains of waters. And God will wipe away every tear from their eyes."

REVELATION 7:16–17

This I declare of the Lord: he alone is my refuge, my place of safety; he is my God, and I trust him. For he will rescue you from every trap and protect you from deadly disease. He will cover you with his feathers. He will shelter you with his wings. His faithful promises are your armor and protection.

PSALM 91:2–4 NLT

We are hard-pressed on every side, yet not crushed; we are perplexed, but not in despair; persecuted, but not forsaken; struck down, but not destroyed.

2 CORINTHIANS 4:8

"Do not fear, little flock, for it is your Father's good pleasure to give you the kingdom."

LUKE 12:32

You also be patient. Establish your hearts, for the coming of the Lord is at hand.

JAMES 5:8

Therefore, having been justified by faith, we have peace with God through our Lord Jesus Christ, through whom also we have access by faith into this grace in which we stand, and rejoice in hope of the glory of God. And not only that, but we also glory in tribulations, knowing that tribulation produces perseverance; and perseverance, character; and character, hope.

ROMANS 5:1–4

"Let not your heart be troubled; you believe in God, believe also in Me. In My Father's house are many mansions; if it were not so, I would have told you. I go to prepare a place for you. And if I go and prepare a place for you, I will come again and receive you to Myself; that where I am, there you may be also."

JOHN 14:1–3

So also Christ died only once as a sacrifice to take away the sins of many people. He will come again but not to deal with our sins again. This time he will bring salvation to all those who are eagerly waiting for him.

HEBREWS 9:28 NLT

"Behold I am coming soon! My reward is with me, and I will give to everyone according to what he has done."

REVELATION 22:12 NLT

"And lo, I am with you always, even to the end of the age."

MATTHEW 28:20b

Appendix A
THE GOSPEL

The word gospel means good news. The Gospel of Jesus Christ is so simple that even a child can understand it, yet so complex that you could spend a lifetime pondering it. The Good News is basically that eternal life is a free gift! *"For God so loved the world that He gave His only begotten Son, that whoever believes in Him should not perish but have everlasting life"* (John 3:16).

God is love and offers us heaven as a free gift; it is never earned or deserved, because we can never be good enough. God is also just and cannot let sin go unpunished. *The wages of sin is death* (Romans 6:23). Since every one of us has sinned, we cannot save ourselves from this judgment of death. The Ten Commandments were given to show us that we could never be good enough. And without Christ's sacrifice covering us, even our good deeds are like filthy rags to Him.

So although God must punish sin, He loves us and doesn't want to punish us. Jesus Christ is the answer to this predicament. Jesus is God who came to Earth, lived a perfect life, and paid for our sins by His horrendous death on the cross. Jesus paid our penalty and, by faith, we can accept His substitution and free offer of eternal life. Our sins are covered by His righteousness; those in the past as well as the future. *We are made right in God's sight when we trust in Jesus Christ to take away our sins. And we all can be saved in this same way, no matter who we are or what we have done* (Romans 3:22 NLT).

Enter heaven by Jesus Christ or condemn yourself to hell, there's no simpler way to put it. *"He that believes in him is not condemned, but he that doesn't believe is condemned already because he has not believed in the name of the only begotten Son of God"* (John 3:18 NLT). Not Allah, Mohammed, the Virgin Mary, Maitreya, the Antichrist, or any other fake god that lost man can think up.

Jesus also conquered death at the Resurrection, where He now stands at the right hand of the Father until the time is ripe for His Second Coming. With thankful hearts, we wait patiently until we are resurrected to reign with God and fellowship together forever.

Believe on the Lord Jesus Christ and you shall be saved (Acts 16:31). This, indeed, is good—no—*great* news!

Appendix B
THE PRAYER OF SALVATION

If you see the hand of God in the events around you and now realize that He is real…If you realize that you're a sinner without a way to save yourself…If you believe the Gospel message that Jesus took your place of punishment on the cross and rose from the dead…If you want the strength and inner peace of knowing God…If you want to be saved from eternal death… If you want to accept God's offer of everlasting life…

Then sincerely, out loud, say the following prayer and God will hear you and will save you, from that very moment:

> Lord God, I open my heart and invite you inside to be my God, to be my Savior, and to be my Friend. I know that I am a sinner and believe you died for my sins on the cross. Forgive me of my sins and wash me clean, for I have decided this day to follow you, Jesus. From this day forward, I'm yours. Help me to live for you. Thank you. In Jesus' name, Amen!

For if you confess with your mouth that Jesus is Lord and believe it in your heart that God raised him from the dead, you will be saved.

ROMANS 10:9

"I am the door; if anyone enters by Me, he will be saved."

JOHN 10:9A

If you just prayed that prayer from your heart, congratulations! You are now a citizen of the Kingdom of Heaven! The angels just sang in joy for your salvation! A sheep that was lost is now found. The Father is happy another prodigal child has come home. Stay strong because the finish line is in sight! Now go tell someone about your decision. I'm looking forward to meeting you on the Other Side.

Appendix C
FEAR NOT AFFIRMATIONS

He is the First and Last, the Beginning and the End!

He is the Keeper of Creation and the Creator of all!

He is the Architect of the Universe and the Manager of Time.

He always was, He always is, and He always will be –

Unmoved, unchanged, undefeated and never undone!

He was bruised and brought healing!

He was pierced and eased pain!

He was persecuted and brought freedom!

He was dead and brought life!

He is risen and brings power!

He reigns and brings peace!

The world can't understand Him,

The armies can't defeat Him,

The schools can't explain Him, and

The leaders can't ignore Him.

Herod couldn't kill Him,

The Pharisees couldn't confuse Him, and

The people couldn't hold Him!

Nero couldn't crush Him,

Hitler couldn't silence Him,

The New Age can't dismiss Him, and

Mohammed can't replace Him!

He is light, love, longevity, and Lord.

He is goodness, kindness, gentleness, and God.

He is holy, righteous, mighty, powerful, and pure.

His ways are right,

His word is eternal,

His will is unchanging, and

His mind is on me!

He is my Redeemer,

He is my Savior,
He is my Guide, and
He is my peace!
He is my joy,
He is my comfort,
He is my Lord, and
He rules my life!
I serve Him because His bond is love,
His burden is light, and
His goal for me is abundant life.
I follow Him because He is
The wisdom of the wise,
The power of the powerful,
The ancient of days, the ruler of rulers,
The leader of leaders,
The overseer of the overcomers, and
The sovereign Lord of all that was
and is and is to come.
And if that seems impressive to you, try this ...
His goal is a relationship with ME!
He will never leave me,
Never forsake me,
Never mislead me,
Never forget me,
Never overlook me, and
Never cancel my appointment
in His appointment book!
When I fall, He lifts me up!
When I fail, He forgives!
When I am weak, He is strong!
When I am lost, He is the way!
When I am afraid, He is my courage!
When I stumble, He steadies me!
When I am hurt, He heals me!

When I am broken, He mends me!
When I am blind, He leads me!
When I am hungry, He feeds me!
When I face trials, He is with me!
When I face persecution, he shields me!
When I face problems, He comforts me!
When I face loss, He provides for me!
When I face Death, He carries me home!
He is everything for everybody, everywhere,
every time and every way.
He is God; He is faithful.
I am His, and He is mine!
My Father in heaven can
whip the father of this world.
So, if you're wondering why I feel so secure,
understand this:
He said it and that settles it.
God is in control, I am on His side, and
That means all is well with my soul.
Every day is a blessing because God IS!

AUTHOR UNKNOWN

Appendix D
EXODUS PACK CHECKLIST

Keep packed and ready to go:

- [ ] Full canteen or two bottles of water (keep the empty bottles!)
- [ ] Water purification tablets
- [ ] Leatherman tool (includes knife, saw, can opener, pliers, screwdriver)
- [ ] Change of clothes x2, include short-sleeve, long-sleeve, pants, socks, underwear
- [ ] Extra pair of walking shoes
- [ ] Cloak or hoodie, rain poncho
- [ ] Bandana or scarf, dust mask
- [ ] Hat
- [ ] Flint, matches and lighter in waterproof container
- [ ] Small LED flashlight with extra batteries
- [ ] Knife (honing stone optional)
- [ ] 100 ft. Paracord
- [ ] Compass and maps
- [ ] Fishing line and hooks
- [ ] Bar of soap, washcloth
- [ ] Travel-size first aid kit (alcohol wipes, gauze pads/tape, band-aids, tweezers, ointment)
- [ ] Disaster antidotes (activated charcoal, potassium iodide tablets)
- [ ] Important documents (copy of passport/ I.D.), few photos of loved ones
- [ ] Sleeping bag and mat
- [ ] Compact Bible, field guide, and notebook/pen
- [ ] 8x10 waterproof tarp, large plastic trash bag
- [ ] Mess kit (cooking pan/pot, plate, cup, fork, spoon, knife, salt)
- [ ] Food: trail mix (dried fruit, nuts, cereal), MRE/freeze-dried packages, jerky
- [ ] Tea bags and/or coffee

- ☐ Toilet paper
- ☐ Currency of the day (jewelry, cash, debit card, oil)
- ☐ Whistle (if you can't do it yourself)
- ☐ Sewing kit
- ☐ Small mirror
- ☐ Keys to a house, car, safe deposit, etc.
- ☐ Medications or special hygiene items
- ☐ Gun (.22 caliber for availability of ammunition)
- ☐ "Quiet" weapon (mace, bow and arrow, or the next two tools below)
- ☐ Cable saw
- ☐ Small machete
- ☐ Personal items (lip balm, lotion, harmonica, memento, whiskey, etc.)
- ☐ Small wind-up radio
- ☐ Small tent (if you can carry it)

Appendix E
OUTFITTING A HOMESTEAD

If you are blessed with a home on some acreage, or are looking to obtain one, here are a few suggestions:

- Situated on at least three acres of higher ground
- Available pasture and timber
- Far enough from urban centers and highways
- Fresh water features, e.g. spring, creek, lake, pond, cistern, well, rain barrel
- Two horses, a milking cow/goat, four egg-laying hens, one rooster, one dog
- Vegetable and herb garden, preferably with a retractable cover or greenhouse
- Minimal gun laws; favorable zoning; low taxes
- Fireplace or wood stove with a covered supply of firewood
- Hurricane lanterns with extra oil; candles
- Shelter for disasters: basement; a rustic cabin off the grid; tree fort or blind
- Pantry stocked with nonperishable food: rice, beans, dried fruit, peanut butter, sugar, salt, tea, coffee, oil, jerky, honey, canned meats, powdered milk, flour, bouillon, jam, flour, as well as paper goods, first aid items, soap, blankets
- Tools, including axe, pick, shovel, hand drill, knife, saw, hammer, broom, wrench, bucket
- Extra gasoline or fuel
- Tarps and heavy-duty tape
- Animal feed, hay, supplies
- Separate barn, chicken coop
- Room enough to house an additional family, if in need
- Bicycles; small boat
- Bury a cache of necessities

- Weapons and ammunition to defend it
- Establish three routes to your retreat; make sure family members know the way

ACKNOWLEDGMENTS

This book is the culmination of many years of study and prodding by God. I would like to thank the following people who've been with me on this journey.

For those closest to me, for their love and support:
My husband, Vincent Benedetto; children, Luke and Jennifer Benedetto; Genevieve and Chase Cook

For good friends and family, for their feedback with minimal eye-rolling:
Mark Wm. Skowron; Andrea and Paul Peralta; Peggy and Gary Monzillo; Brenda and Gary Cook; Kathleen Rodriguez; Tim Johnson; Joyce Finnegan

For my teachers, for their wisdom:
JD Farag; Hal Lindsey; Ed Hindson; Charles Stanley; David Jeremiah; Mark Hitchcock; Chuck Smith; Billy Graham; Keith Green; Chris Tomlin; D. James Kennedy; Bob Coy; Greg Laurie; Arno Froese; John F. Walvoord; Grant Jeffrey; Tim LaHaye; Ray Comfort; Donna Wasson; RaptureReady.com

For various and sundry reasons:
Anna and Vincent Monaco; Joan and Nick Benedetto; Irwin Hart; Rita Conyers; Mike Gallagher; Kevin Martin; JRR Tolkien; Rose Shulman; Shelley Lake; William Joyner; John Roberts; Ira Litzenblatt

For believing in this book and publishing it:
Bill Carmichael and the staff at Deep River Books

And last but not least:
All to the Lord Jesus Christ, for the glory of God!

ABOUT THE AUTHOR

Pat Benedetto has been a student of Bible prophecy for thirty-nine years.

As a teenager, she set out on a search for the Truth, which ultimately led her to the Bible. While working for the local newspaper, Pat noticed that current events were eerily similar to biblical prophecies, which sparked a lifelong passion for God and eschatology. She humbly admits that miracles in her life have strengthened her faith beyond all doubt.

After graduating from Taylor Business Institute in New York City, Pat worked as an editor's assistant before moving to Florida and into the graphic arts field. She currently manages the graphics department of a large financial corporation.

Pat is married to her childhood sweetheart, Vincent, and they have two happily married children and a new grandson. They attend Calvary Chapel.

Pat spends her free time looking up!

NOTE

Every effort has been made to determine that all illustrations and quotations are royalty-free or public domain. Permissions for Scripture quotations are on the title page, as required.

The author and publisher disclaims any responsibility for any loss, injury or damages caused as a result of any of the activities or the use of the survival techniques described in this book. Readers are advised to read and follow usage instructions included with any survival products that they buy.

The world is changing by the day, and it's been a challenge to put down all prophetic events in this book. If you would like to study this subject further, please read the Bible—the ultimate source—as well as prophecy and survival materials, which are available at your local bookstore, library, or online.

Visit www.facebook.com/survivingthetribulation
or contact the author at
survivingthetribulation@yahoo.com

*"I am the Alpha and the Omega,
the First and the Last,
the Beginning and the End."*
JESUS CHRIST

ENDNOTES

Introduction

    1. *Merriam-Webster's Collegiate Dictionary,* Tenth Edition. (Springfield: Merriam-Webster, Inc., 1993), p. 1260.

Chapter 2

    1. Flavius Josephus, *The Complete Works–Antiquities of the Jews,* translated by William Whiston; Book 18, Chapter 3, Section 3, Verses 63-64. (Peabody: Hendrickson Publishers, 1987), p. 480.

Chapter 3

    1. Lambert Dolphin, "World Population Since Creation," accessed February 12, 2015, http://ldolphin.org/popul.html.

    2. Kevin Johnson, "USA TODAY," (April 29, 2012), accessed February 18, 2015, from Police Executive Research Forum, http://policeforum.org.

Chapter 5

    1. Carol Brooks, "The United Nations," attributing quote to Paul Henri-Spaak addressing the EU Economic Summit (1945), accessed February 18, 2015 http://inplainsite.org/html/the_united_nations.html.

Chapter 10

    1. John Muir, "Atlantic Monthly," (January 1869), accessed February 18, 2015, http://quotationspage.com.

Chapter 12

    1. FEMA, *Protection in the Nuclear Age,* (Washington, DC: June 12, 1985), p. 18.

2. United States Nuclear Regulatory Commission, "FAQ About Potassium Iodide," accessed February 18, 2015, http://www.nrc.gov/about-nrc/emerg-preparedness/aboutemerg-preparedness/potassium-iodide/ki-faq.html.
3. EMR Labs, "Activated Charcoal Universal Antidote," accessed February 18, 2015, http://quantumbalancing.com/activatedcharcoal.htm.